SEX AND SEXUALITY IN BROADCASTING

BROADCASTING STANDARDS COUNCIL

5-8 The Sanctuary
London SW1P 3JS

Tel: 071-233 0544
Fax: 071-233 0397

SEX AND SEXUALITY IN BROADCASTING

Andrea Millwood Hargrave

BROADCASTING STANDARDS COUNCIL
PUBLIC OPINION AND BROADCASTING STANDARDS – 3

John Libbey
JL
LONDON · PARIS · ROME

British Library Cataloguing in Publication Data

Sex and Sexuality in Broadcasting
  I. Hargrave, Andrea Millwood
  384.54

ISSN: 0960-3999
ISBN: 0 86196 393 8

Published by

John Libbey & Company Ltd, 13 Smiths Yard, Summerley Street,
London SW18 4HR, England
Telephone: 081-947 2777 – Fax: 081-947 2664
John Libbey Eurotext Ltd, 6 rue Blanche, 92120 Montrouge, France
John Libbey - C.I.C. s.r.l., via Lazzaro Spallanzani 11, 00161 Rome, Italy

Printed in Great Britain by Whitstable Litho Ltd, Whitstable, Kent, U.K.

Contents

Foreword

My colleagues and I on the Council have seen it as one of our prime tasks to ensure the regular provision of high-quality research into the matters which fall within our remit. Only in this way can we hope to ground our conclusions about the radio and television programmes serving the public in this country on a realistic understanding of their audiences' attitudes and moods.

It is in this way too that we make our contribution to the continuing debate about broadcasting and its values.

In previous years, the Council's Annual Reviews have dealt with violence in television fiction and with issues of taste and decency, including the constantly controversial topic of bad language which generates more complaints than almost anything else. The theme chosen in 1992, Sex & Sexuality, is also one which arouses strong feelings. As in 1991, the findings of the Council's research are included in the Review and accompanied by essays from a number of broadcasting practitioners and others expressing their personal views on the subject. We hope that all those who read the Review, from whatever perspective they regard it, will find it interesting and challenging.

Lord Rees Mogg
Chairman, Broadcasting Standards Council

Introduction

The attitudes of the viewing and listening public to the depiction of sexual activity and the portrayal of sexuality in broadcasting is an area that would appear to have been little explored. Some data are available describing, in broad outline, opinions about the fact that sex is depicted on television at all, but there seems to be no real consideration of the factors that shape these views, nor a perspective on the experiences the audience has while watching or listening to such material. Rather more research has been conducted (primarily in the United States) which has considered the actual portrayal of sexual activity on television. This work has taken the form of content analyses which have monitored the type of sex depicted, the participants, the scene, the programme genre and – in some cases – the transmission time. However, this methodology is factual and allows a purely objective consideration of what is already on screen. There is no room in content analyses for understanding what the audience's reaction might be. There has also been some research surveying the portrayal of sexuality – but again, this has tended to take the form of factual surveys.

The Broadcasting Standards Council is required, as part of the remit granted to it in 1988, to monitor, undertake research and report on the portrayal of sex in broadcasting, as well as violence and matters of taste and decency. This Annual Review, considering the depiction of sex and sexuality in broadcasting, is the third in a series of comprehensive studies which have considered the major parts of the Council's remit. It is designed to answer questions about the attitudes of the audience, to survey programme output and to inform the Council's function to consider complaints.

A further consideration has been the deregulation of television and the burgeoning choice of television channels available to those who choose to buy the relevant receiving equipment. There are already channels available that deal exclusively in erotica, and others that may be considered to go beyond. While they cater for a minority audience, it is important that the Council understands the reactions of the viewer to depictions of sexual activity in mainstream broadcasting.

Previous research commissioned by the Council has shown that, although respondents said that they were most concerned about the portrayal of violence and the use of bad language in television programmes, the viewing of sexual material was the most-often cited reason for turning the television off, regardless of the composition of the audience with whom one was watching. The respondents expressed, variously, embarrassment or offence or a desire to protect others, for example, children. One of the key tasks of this research then, was to explore the tension that is exposed between an acceptance that sexual activity on television was not a cause for worry and the realization that it could create great discomfort.

Certain questions needed to be answered. What are the audience's reactions to the material already available? Previous research had found that there were contextual considerations which most people accepted and made while they were watching or listening to broadcasts. One of the results of such deliberations might well lead to the television or radio being switched off. What are the contextual considerations for sexual material? How can the broadcaster ensure the audience is not driven away unnecessarily but is given adequate advance information to make judgements about programmes?

What are the differences between groups of people? Is gender a key discriminator of attitude, or age, or social class, or lifestyle? What are the issues that affect different people and how can the broadcaster allow for these differences? What, if any, are the differences in attitude to male and female homosexuality and why do they exist? Are the issues about sexuality only of interest or concern to the homosexual viewer or listener?

The Council used a variety of techniques to explore these questions. The research methodology had to be devised to take account of the particular sensitivities that respondents might bring to a consideration of sex on television. The research programme therefore included both qualitative and quantitative elements (for details see Appendix 5). A wide-ranging series of group discussions, including some with homosexual respondents, took place as well as a set of family interviews (in which children and their parents were interviewed separately at first then brought together for a joint interview). The Council has used this last technique very successfully in the past as a means of understanding the specific dynamics within the family as a viewing unit.

The qualitative research fed in to the design of the quantitative study in which 1137 respondents, aged 13 and over, took part. In addition the Council commissioned a content analysis of one week's terrestrial television programming.

The Review presents the issues which the depiction of sex on television raises and the way respondents react to such portrayals. Examples of hypothetical scenarios, each exploring different facets of the portrayal of sex, were considered. The particular demands of the homosexual viewer, a minority group determined by its sexuality, are presented as well as the findings of the content analysis. Finally the Council presents a series of essays from people both within and outside the British broadcasting industry, each considering the role of sexual material in broadcasting.

1 The issue of sex on television

Violence, sex and bad language on television

As has already been mentioned, this research showed that the majority (66 per cent) of respondents considered there was too much violence on television and nearly that number considered there was too much bad language. About two in five respondents thought that the level of sexual activity depicted was too high (see Table 1).[1]

Table 1. Amount of violence, sex and bad language on television

	Too much %	Right amount %	Too little %
Violence	66	32	2
Sex	41	54	4
Bad language	60	38	2

On closer examination (see Appendix 1) it can be seen that those respondents who were older, and female respondents, were more likely to say that the amount of violence, bad language and sexual activity on television was 'too much'. The tables also show that parents' levels of concern seemed to vary depending on the age of their children.

Respondents also expressed a general belief that standards of broadcasting were becoming more liberal and depictions of sex more explicit. The questionnaire asked respondents to consider how much sex they thought was shown on television now in comparison with some time previously (undefined). As Table 2 below shows, in

---

1 Unless otherwise specified, all tabular data presented in this Review are based on a nationally representative survey conducted for the Broadcasting Standards Council by the British Market Research Bureau in April 1992. All data are based on a sample of 1137 respondents.

general, respondents felt that there was more sex on television, and a substantial number of respondents of all ages thought that there was a lot more.

Table 2. Amount of sex on television these days

	Lot more	Little more	Same amount	Little less	Lot less
	%	%	%	%	%
Total	43	28	20	5	3
Age of respondent					
13–17	34	32	21	8	5
18–24	25	37	25	7	6
25–34	38	34	17	7	3
35–54	44	30	19	4	3
55+	56	17	18	5	3

Respondents mentioned instances in which they felt these changes had occurred and barriers had been pushed back (such as in *A Time To Dance*, the dramatization on television of Melvyn Bragg's novel). There was a belief that, once a boundary had been breached, it would disappear for all time and this was not necessarily welcomed. There was a concern about sudden or rapid change and a feeling that this was not altogether desirable.

> *'The borderline of decency is being pushed, and gradually a change of attitudes is being forced on society until it's accepted as normal. That's a problem, that's a shame.'*
> (55+, male, Bristol)

Many respondents expressed the view that the current levels of explicitness were quite adequate.

In order to see if respondents' reactions to the amount of violence, sex and bad language on television affected the concern they might feel about the depiction of these, respondents were asked to say which, if any, of these three areas most concerned them. Over half (56 per cent) said that they were most concerned about the violence shown on television, while one in five said they were most concerned about the amount of bad language. Twelve per cent said that the portrayal of sexual activity was of most concern to them while another ten per cent said that none of these was of particular concern.

In summary then, the depiction of sexual activity would seem to create few problems insofar as respondents admitted to little concern about it. Nonetheless, as we will see, the ability of such depictions to embarrass or offend is greater than for either violence or bad language.

The influence of television

> *'The media is responsible. With all this rape that is going on, TV has a lot to answer for, and marriages breaking up'.*
> *(55+, male, Bristol)*

The continuing debate about broadcasting's potential influence on the viewer or listener and, in turn, on the way in which society conducts itself is explored again in this Review. As in previous years, the Council asked questions about the perceived influence (both positive and negative) of television, and full results are given in Appendix 2. Only those statements relating specifically to attitudes about the influence of television on social issues or in sexual matters are considered here.

Table 3. Perceived influences of television

	Extremely strong influence	Strong influence	Some influence	Not much influence	No influence
	%	%	%	%	%
Helping children make sense of social problems	12	30	41	13	4
Encouraging sexual and moral permissiveness	12	24	35	19	9

As the statements in Table 3 above show, most respondents thought that television could have a positive effect on children, by helping them understand and make sense of social problems. Although these 'social problems' were undefined in the quantitative section of the study, the qualitative research would suggest they are likely to include issues that arise from the depiction of, or are consequences of, sexual activity (such as teenage pregnancy or AIDS). Indeed nearly 60 per cent of the younger respondents in the quantitative study (those aged 17 and under) felt that television had an 'extremely strong' influence in this area (in comparison with 42 per cent of the sample as a whole).

The statement that television can 'encourage sexual or moral permissiveness' was particularly supported by older respondents (those aged 55 and over). Nearly 60 per cent said that television had a 'strong' or 'extremely strong' influence here in comparison with just over a third of the sample as whole. Respondents aged 17 and under did not agree with this by and large however, and neither did parents. Indeed, the data show that being a parent had very little effect on the respondent's perception of the influence of television.

Despite this finding that parenthood as a variable in the quantitative study did not appear to affect respondents' attitudes to the perceived influences of television, there did appear to be a change in the attitudes expressed when respondents were questioned simply as individuals (as in the quantitative study or in group discussions) and when they were asked to consider issues *as parents* (as in the family interviews). In the latter role, more concern was expressed about the possible influence of television. It was something that parents felt they had to keep their eye on.

'You see it getting more and more explicit. You wonder where it will end up'.
(Mother, BC1 Family with children 16–19, Thames Valley)

'I wouldn't be happy with more explicit sex on the telly, there's more than enough.
Not for the effect it would have on young people, they're getting videos already.
There's nothing you can do about that.'
(Mother, C2D Family with Children 12–15, London)

Respondents to the questionnaire were also asked to consider a series of attitude statements designed to investigate opinions about a variety of issues surrounding the presentation of sex on television. Included within this battery were some additional attitudinal statements about the possible (negative) effect of showing sex scenes on televison. As Table 4 shows, respondents were fairly equally divided between those that agreed and those that disagreed with the statements 'Showing sex only encourages the young to experiment too soon' and 'Showing sex encourages immoral behaviour'. Importantly however, nearly two in five respondents agreed that they found the depiction of sexual activity offensive, and this increased to 40 per cent of those aged 55 and over agreeing strongly (in comparison with 18 per cent of the sample as a whole).

Table 4. The negative influence of television

	Strongly agree %	Slightly agree %	Slightly disagree %	Strongly disagree %
Showing sex only encourages the young to experiment too soon	28	28	24	19
Showing sex scenes on television encourages immoral behaviour	21	27	27	24
I find it offensive to see sex scenes on television	18	21	30	31

Certain of the attitude statements considered whether sex scenes on television served an educative role by exposing people to sex and encouraging the discussion of sexual matters. As Table 5 shows, many respondents were likely to agree that issues such as 'safe sex' should be addressed on television and sex scenes should lead 'by example'. Younger respondents (those aged under 25) were significantly more likely to 'agree strongly' with the statement 'It should be implied that condoms are used in sex scenes these days to encourage 'safe sex' – 59 per cent of those aged under 25 agreed strongly with this in comparison with 43 per cent of the general sample. There was also agreement that sex scenes might encourage discussion with parents while the youngest of the respondents, aged 17 and under, were particularly likely to agree with the statement 'Showing sex is a good way of educating children in the facts of life' (62 per cent of the younger respondents agreed in comparison with 45 per cent of the total sample). Conversely, the older respondents, aged 55 and over, were significantly more likely to *disagree* with this statement (42 per cent strongly disagreed in comparison with 28 per cent of the sample as a whole). There was also less agreement in this age group with the statement which suggested it was good to show sex on television because this encouraged general discussion.

Table 5. Television's educative role

	Strongly agree %	Slightly agree %	Slightly disagree %	Strongly disagree %
It should be implied that condoms are used in sex scenes these days to encourage 'safe sex'	43	38	10	9
Sex scenes give parents a good chance to talk about these things with their children	10	43	26	21
Showing sex is a good way of helping to educate children in the facts of life	10	35	26	28
It's good to show sex as it encourages people to talk about it	8	39	31	22

General attitudes to sex on television

The vast majority of respondents (88 per cent) agreed with the statement 'People who don't like watching sex can always switch off'. This echoed a comment from one of the group discussions:

> 'To me nobody makes you watch these things ... sometimes I think people go a bit over the top when they say this shouldn't be on and that shouldn't be on because you can turn it off, nobody actually makes you watch these things.'
> (35–45, female, Manchester)

A similarly large number of respondents (78 per cent) agreed with the comment 'If people want to watch sex on television, they should be allowed to'. Nonetheless it was felt that programmes which showed supposed sexual activity had to abide by certain codes and there were considerations which made them more acceptable; for example, if the sexual activity occurred within 'a loving relationship'. Parents were found to agree with this particular statement slightly more than the sample as a whole, reflecting, perhaps, their concerns that all role models should be 'good' ones. (Later in the Review, we consider specific fictitious examples of scenes that might be shown on television.)

Table 6. General opinions about sex scenes on television

	Strongly agree %	Slightly agree %	Slightly disagree %	Strongly disagree %
People who don't like watching sex can always switch off	65	23	5	7
If people want to watch sex on TV, they should be allowed to	38	40	13	9
Showing sex is OK if it's seen to be in a loving relationship	25	45	18	11
It's alright to show sex because it is what people do in everyday life	14	37	28	21
European TV is better because it has a more open attitude to sex	37	28	31	33

Some respondents commented on the perceived greater openness of European tele-vision, particularly in sexual matters, and some male respondents argued that this displayed a healthier attitude than that of the British.

> 'We don't like to see men showing affection towards each other in this country. Though perhaps that's not always a good thing ... We're reluctant to show physical affection here ... we do it by the use of words ... you say 'you bastard' to a friend and it's a term of verbal affection'.
> (35–45, male, Slough)

Women over 55 years of age were more likely to be against the depiction of sex on television. They often explained this in terms of the way they had been brought up:

> 'You see, the younger generation they don't respect each other's bodies ... they think they are there to be used.'
> (55+, female, Bristol)

> 'Sex is for general conversation now, they (younger people) aren't embarrassed ... I couldn't have asked my mother anything, she'd have been embarrased.'
> (55+, female, Bristol)

> 'Now I'll go in to the other room if the youngsters ... my son is in his twenties ... want to watch it. My kids think I'm a prude. They say I'm old-fashioned. Well I'll stay old-fashioned ... and sometimes it gets to heated arguments.'
> (55+, female, Cambs/Lincs Borders)

And they recognized that younger generations did not necessarily feel the same, but were not sure greater openness was a positive thing.

> 'There's too much sex on TV ... and there's sex education at school and they (young people) are influenced by the television and it's bad ... it's making youngsters too promiscuous...and sex becomes detached from love.'
> (55+, female, Bristol)

'I never heard my mother tell me anything ... but where's it leading to? More rape, more abuse of children, AIDS.'
(55+, female, Bristol)

Younger respondents themselves realized that the older generations were embarrassed or found such material distasteful.

Respondents aged under 55 were more tolerant of the depiction of sex (although women were still more conservative than men). There was a slight feeling from the qualitative research, however, that the under 25 year olds were more conservative than those aged between 25 and 50. Although these younger respondents were loathe to admit to a desire for censorship and claimed to take a libertarian view of broadcasting, they were less radical in what they found acceptable.

'Personally I don't want to see lesbianism but I don't want to stop things being televised. You could show what you like after 12.00 (midnight).'

(Another) 'Yes, I don't agree with censorship. You can just turn it off. I hate it when they cut bits out of films. It's up to you to turn it off. Rape scenes or child abuse I wouldn't want to watch it myself but I don't object to showing it.'
(18–19, females, Sheffield)[2]

There is some suggestion that it is this group that has been most affected by the threat of AIDS and their attitudes might have reflected this.

Table 7. Television's policy

	Strongly agree %	Slightly agree %	Slightly disagree %	Strongly disagree %
Scenes of violent sex such as rape should never be shown on TV	47	18	20	15
You can show more explicit sex scenes on video than on broadcast TV	39	34	12	15
It's important to show sex scenes if they're necessary to the story	23	42	20	15
It's alright to show just one sex scene, but not if it's all the way through the programme	21	40	23	16
The broadcasters have a very clear policy about what can be shown in sex scenes	20	40	26	13
I sometimes feel uncertain about how far broadcasters should go when showing sex scenes on television	17	44	25	13
There's too much sex shown on television these days	28	27	29	16
It's OK to show sex on television because you know the couple are only acting	8	27	33	32

---

2   This, and other quotes similarly presented, are spoken by different respondents in a group.

Respondents also commented on some issues of policy (see Table 7). Most respondents agreed 'You can show more explicit sex scenes on video than on broadcast television'. Older respondents were more likely to agree 'There is too much sex shown on television these days' and were less likely to concur with the statement 'It's important to show sex scenes if they're necessary to the story'. Nearly two out of three respondents also agreed that 'Scenes of violent sex such as rape should never be shown on television'. Respondents aged over 55 were particularly likely to agree strongly with this statement (61 per cent agreeing strongly in comparison with 47 per cent of the general sample).

It should also be noted that, on the whole, many respondents felt that broadcasters had a clear policy about the depiction of sexual activity, although the policy did not always reflect the respondent's own feelings about the subject.

Reasons for offence

Nearly two in five adults said that they had switched off or changed channels when watching television with children aged 15 years and under. This increased to nearly half of those parents with children living at home.

The principal reasons cited for turning the television off or changing channels was the portrayal of sexual activity (33 per cent of mentions), bad language (28 per cent) and violence (27 per cent). As has been found in previous BSC research, although violence and bad language cause the most concern when shown on television, depicted sexual activity created the most offence. Such offence was however, relatively infrequent – the majority of respondents (80 per cent) who had viewed television with a child and had turned it off or changed channels said that they had done so less than three times in the previous six months.

Nearly one-half of the offending programmes had been transmitted in the hour before the Watershed (8.00 pm to 9.00 pm) while another 31 per cent had been broadcast between 9.00 and 10.00 pm. Table 8 below shows those programme categories in which the offensive item occurred.

Table 8. Programmes causing respondents to turn television off/change channels when viewing with 15 year olds and younger

Programme category	%
Films	55
Drama	35
Soap operas	15
Documentaries	13
Comedies	11

Respondents were also asked to consider whether or not they had turned the television off or changed channels because they had felt personal disgust at what they saw. Of the sample as a whole, just over one-quarter said that they had done so. When older respondents were considered in isolation, 40 per cent said they had turned off or switched channels. The reasons for offence were the portrayal of sexual activity (offence was particularly great among the over 55 year olds – nearly two in five of this group said they had taken action when watching such programming in comparison with 26 per cent of the sample as a whole). Other reasons were bad language (mentioned by a quarter of the respondents) and violence (mentioned by just over one in five interviewees).

Of those who listened to the radio, three per cent said that they had been personally disgusted by an item on the radio and the prime reason for offence was political opinion or debate.

Again, the findings above reflect the embarrassment or offence many respondents could feel when watching scenes on television portraying sexual activity. This contrasts with their overall attitude to the issue of sex, which suggested a more relaxed approach to this area of the Council's remit than others.

2 The special problems of parents

Issues of responsibility

As has already been mentioned, when questioned as individuals *for their own opinions*, or interviewed as part of a group discussion with their peers, parents could shrug off their mantle of parenthood and answer questions in a way which reflected their homogeneity within that group. However, in the family interviews, they saw themselves as part of the family unit and displayed quite a different set of attitudes towards broadcasting.

The importance of the 9.00 pm Watershed has already been mentioned. In the hours before the Watershed, a greater number of parents felt that the broadcaster should assume sole or joint responsibility for the suitability of material that might be transmitted to a child audience. After the Watershed, more parents were prepared to take on sole responsibility for their children's viewing.

Table 9. Responsibility for broadcast – the parents' view

	Broadcaster %	Parent %	Both %
Pre-Watershed	15	72	13
Post-Watershed	9	86	5

Base: 410 respondents.

Indeed, parents were very concerned in general that they should have control over what their children watched. Theoretically they expressed the hope (in the qualitative research) that they would monitor and make decisions on the appropriateness or otherwise of programmes for their children. However, they accepted that such rigorous monitoring was only possible in the most extreme of cases. 'Bedtime' was the means most used as a way of drawing children away from material they did not want them to watch. Parents would often *'fudge an issue or hope it goes away'*.

> *'If they ask about being able to watch a film, I wouldn't say "no", I would just keep the television on another channel and hope they'll forget'.*
> *(Mother, C2D Family with children 7–11, Liverpool)*

Parents felt strongly that television had a clear responsibility both to themselves and to their children when programmes included material of a demanding nature, such as the discussion of social issues. They felt that questions were sometimes raised that needed a resolution and which they might not have wished to bring up at that point in their child's development. Parents did not always feel they, or their children, were ready to answer or face some of the issues that were addressed. They also said that if issues were raised by the inclusion of sex, in particular, in a programme and these were dealt with *within* that programme (so that the issues were resolved) they could cope with subsequent discussion far more easily.

Grange Hill was mentioned as an example of programming that dealt ably with social issues. The specific example mentioned was teenage pregnancy which was discussed within the programme over a short period of time. Other programmes such as *EastEnders* and *Brookside* were sometimes criticized for the length of time (number of episodes) they took between first raising an issue and then achieving a resolution.

> *'I wish* EastEnders *would get on with this AIDS thing, the kids go on and on about it.'*
> *(Mother, C2D Family with children 12–15, London)*

Parents accepted that their children would 'eventually find out what it's (sex) all about' but they were concerned that their children should not be introduced to sex too early, or before they (the parents) were happy to deal with related issues.

Further, the fact that television came into one's home, an essentially private place, increased parents' feeling of vulnerability. They particularly commented on the fact, in relation to the depiction of sexual activity, that they felt they were being asked to step into the bedroom with actors and that other members of the family were 'stepping into the scene with you'.

> *'I'm not remotely shocked by it, but should the camera go into the bedroom necessarily? Must it dwell on the sexual act quite to that extent? What's it trying to achieve? I end up feeling a bit voyeuristic, which is not a thing I particularly want to feel.'*
> *(Teacher, Secondary school, Nottingham).*

> *'In the old days when one had the so-called romantic scenes, the couple were never seen walking into the room! ... It's pretty obvious what they're going into the bedroom for, so there's no need to go into the gory details.'*
> *(Mother, BC1 Family with children 16–18, Thames Valley)*

Children themselves, as the quantitative results also showed, were less concerned about how far television might go.

> *'You do see more and more now, and I know my mum and dad worry about it, but at the end of the day there's only so far you can go.'*
> *(Daughter, 18, BC1 Family with children 16–19, Thames Valley)*

Parents also mentioned the importance of scheduling conventions and the adequate

15

labelling of programmes as being important devices they could use to avoid material they did not wish their children to see (see also Appendix 3).

Respondents who were over 55 years old commented on the embarrassment they could feel when watching the depiction of sexual activity on television with their grandchildren or, indeed, their children, even if they were adults. In the case of adult offspring, much of the discomfort centered on the reluctant admission that their children were active sexual beings. Once the children had children of their own, this particular embarrassment was felt to lessen, as if the act of procreation had moved the focus away from the passionate side of their children's nature.

Viewing as a family

As previous research has found (Millwood Hargrave, 1991), the context within which one viewed, and the people with whom one viewed, could create particular difficulties. While material may not have been found offensive or embarrassing when viewed alone, when seen with others, it was. This was particularly true where the audience of which one was part was a mixture of generations and sexes.

> 'When other folk are there in the room with you, they get embarrassed because you are there ... but if the youngsters were by themselves they wouldn't be embarrassed.'
> (55+, female, Cambs/Lincs Borders)

> 'If the kids would be watching it on their own together with a friend or whatever they probably wouldn't be embarrassed ... it's because you are there.'
> (35–45, female, Manchester)

> 'Men's Room was serious and I was embarrassed because my parents were in the room. The sex scenes were right explicit, a top shelf job.'
> (18–19, female, Sheffield)

The embarrassment that might be felt became increasingly acute for parents as their awareness of their child's sexual maturity grew.

> 'When there is sex on TV I feel embarrassed because they (his parents) are there ... you know they are looking at you to see your reaction ... they think you are too young ... Mum likes to think of you as her sweet innocent angel ... and they're concerned about you getting into trouble.'
> (16–17, male, Bristol)

The vulnerability that parents felt because they were in their own homes has already been referred to, but should be mentioned again.

> 'It's when you're sitting there, thinking you're safe, and then suddenly something like that (Smith and Jones kissing[3]) hits you. I don't think it's embarrassing itself but it's when you're watching (with the children) that it starts to get uncomfortable'.
> (Father, C2D Family with children 11–15, Middlesex)

These feelings of vulnerability, a desire to do the best by one's children and the peer pressure exerted by one's children's friends all added to some parents' confusion

---

3   For full details of this and other programming clips used in this research, please refer to Appendix 5.

about what their attitudes to sex on television should be. In many of the family interviews, parents appeared to seek a level of 'reassurance' from the researchers:

> *'I'd like to know how we stack up against the others you have interviewed'*
> *(Father, BC1 Family with children 12–15, Liverpool).*

These parents realized that there was nothing intrinsically wrong with the depiction of sex, but they felt it was a private issue which they were not always ready to address with their children at the time at which it presented itself through the television. Again, they felt that adequate labelling and appropriate scheduling could lessen the risk of embarrassment.

> *'Around 9.00 o'clock you can see some explicit sex scenes. I don't know if there are any kids who are influenced by that, or whether it's the adults sitting watching it that are uncomfortable. I suspect the parents ... are embarrassed in case the kids ask a question. And then you have to go into it.'*
> *(Mother, C2D Family with children 12–15, London)*

Parents drew a distinction between 'constructive' references to sex and the depiction of passionate or 'irrational' sex. In the former, television was seen to have an educative role (see also views expressed in Table 5), leading to discussion, adding to the child's knowledge of sexual issues in a responsible way. This was seen as positive and to be building on information provided in schools.

> *'They'll come back from school sex education and say 'they've been on about poofs today but they're not poofs they're homosexuals', and that breaks the ice ... and I want TV to break the ice too: I wouldn't know where to start otherwise ... But it's when they're just humping in some film on telly, that's when I get embarrassed 'cause it's more difficult to know what to say.'*
> *(30–45, male, Sheffield)*

Programmes discussing sexual matters on television allowed difficult topics such as AIDS to be talked about and parents were sometimes grateful that they did not have to raise the issue first. Indeed, some parents said that they used references to sex on television to check whether or not their children understood the 'processes'. Children could, in a similar way, demonstrate their knowledge to their parents (e.g. laughing at 'dirty' jokes).

Television also had a role to play in portraying 'what relationships are like'. This encompassed a 'norm' of early meeting, dating, sexual relationships, models of behaviour as well as offering models of sexuality and role definition. Some respondents talked about the way in which television might legitimize certain behaviour – not always, it was felt, positively.

> *'If that's setting a standard (Ex, showing an unmarried couple in bed together at the man's home, with the children from his previous marriage coming into the bedroom), my fear is that will become the norm – nobody wants to be committed anyway'.*
> *(Social worker, Glasgow)*

Other respondents claimed to be pleased that television often did show that relationships could be problematic.

> *'They (the children) know what a happy marriage is like, they have to find out about*

> *these (other) things somehow, and at least something like* EastEnders *is fairly responsible in what they show.'*
> *(Mother, C2D Family with children 7–11, Liverpool)*

The distinction that parents drew, as already mentioned, was between these 'constructive' references to sex and the depiction of passionate sex. It was this which caused the greatest embarrassment, the more particularly so if the child with whom one was viewing was of the opposite sex.

> *'You just don't feel right if you are sitting there with your daughter and they start humping on the screen'.*
> *(35–50, male)*

> *'You'll be sitting there and something might come on and you just hope it's over very quickly if the children are there'.*
> *(Mother, BC1 Family with children 7–11, BC1, London)*

It seemed that this extreme embarrassment occurred because parents wanted to show themselves to their children as caring, responsible and protective – not with a passionate side to their natures.

Equally, children had great difficulty in seeing their parents as sexual beings, anything other than 'parents' – the portrayal of passionate sex broke a taboo within the conventional parent-child relationship.

> *'You don't like to think of your parents having sex because they're your parents and you see them as protectors ... as making the dinner.'*
> *(20–24, female, Harrow)*

> *'It's as if they had me and that was it. You're brought up to think that way. Underneath it all you know they still do it, but you prefer not to think about it.'*
> *(16–18, male, Bristol)*

Children were likely to claim that embarrassment emanated from their parents and made the viewing situation difficult. They claimed that they themselves were beyond embarrassment.

> *'It goes in one ear and out the other.'*
> *(Son, 18, C2D Family with children, Nottingham)*

> *'I don't know what old people are complaining about, 'cos they must have done it when they were kids.'*
> *(Daughter, 13, C2D Family with children 12–15, Edgware)*

Despite this air of bravado, upon closer questioning, many of the younger respondents would admit they experienced embarrassment on their own account.

> *'I'd hate it. We wouldn't watch that sort of thing together anyway. We've usually got three TVs on at the same time anyway. Or mum would leave.'*
> *(Son, C2D Family with children 16–18, Nottingham).*

These respondents felt they were often required to hide their own sexuality from their parents.

> *'You feel you're right in there with them (the actors). All you want to do is look at*

the wallpaper.'
(Son, 18, C2D Family with children, Nottingham)

'You don't talk to your dad about sex ... my father accepts that it goes on, but you don't open up to him about it ... to him you're his little girl ... so when something sexy comes on he'll make tea or flick over or laugh through embarrassment.'
(20–24, female, Harrow)

Differences in attitudes to the portrayal of sex on television by ages of children

Parents with very young children felt that they could still identify with their recent 'single lives' and they were generally found to be more tolerant about sex scenes in television programming. They accepted that much of this tolerance stemmed from the fact that they were not yet in a position to have to 'do battle' over television viewing with their children. There was a great concern however that they should be 'good' parents – not overly restrictive but setting clear standards. They realized that there was not yet a need for a clear television policy, as their children went to bed early and at regular times.

These parents did express concerns for the future however, when they realized they may have to become more active 'censors'. They were aware that their own viewing of sex on television might be curtailed as their children grew older and increasingly watched television with them. At that point, they knew, they would have to consider their children's presence. These parents felt that they would become more conservative then, despite their memories of their own youth and their avowed desire not to be 'prudish'.

Those parents with children up to about eight years old felt that it was enough that their children had a basic knowledge of sex and that sex was not seen as entertainment. They felt that they would have little requirement to explain anything about sexual activity to their children.

'(Wilt) I saw that, and it was hilarious. I watched it with my eight year old and he wanted a (rubber) doll 'cause he didn't know what it was ... but my 11 year old would know and that would be more embarrassing'.
(30–45, male, Sheffield)

'Eleven and twelve is the age when you have to hammer these issues out, 'cause there's so much knocking about now ... but when they're younger sometimes you can get away without telling them the whole truth.'
(30–45, male, Sheffield)

'When they are young, seven or eight or younger, it is not so embarrassing ... you hope they don't ask but if they do you can be economical with the truth ... well they've taken their clothes off because it must be hot ... but in their teens it's more embarrassing'.
(30–45, female, Harrow)

'We were watching Fatal Attraction *and he's giving her one in the sink and my wife, she didn't know what to do and our seven year old, he thought it was hilarious*

19

... he thought he was washing her backside.'
(30–45, male, Sheffield)

Some concern was expressed about programmes such as *Neighbours*, which were seen to appeal to the young and which were felt to be dealing, increasingly, with adult issues. Some – limited – concern was also voiced about gender stereotyping, particularly in advertisements.

As has already been indicated, parents with children of this age still felt that they could 'fudge' issues if they wanted to. They felt that television exerted a limited effect on their children; the playground and their children's peers being more important influences.

'If she understands it, she won't say anything. If she doesn't understand it, she won't
say anything. It's just if she thinks she should know about it that she might ask.'
(Mother, C2D Family with children 7–11, Liverpool)

Greater discomfort was expressed by parents as their children approached puberty (often at about the age of eleven). Television then started to become a legitimate vehicle for raising issues. Children in this age group also were beginning to become more aware of the world around them, and were increasingly cognizant of the fact that their parents might be exerting a greater control over their viewing than they would like.

'I would like to see a programme about how babies come out, because I can't get
anyone to explain it to me, and I'm scared that it will come as too much of a shock
when I'm older.'
(Daughter, 9, BC1 Family with children, London)

Meanwhile, this group of parents, with children approaching their teens, was now more comfortable watching sex scenes with their own parents. As has been suggested before, it was as if their own sexuality was now admitted, as they had themselves become parents.

The research suggested that it was parents of children aged between 11 and 15 who found the issues surrounding the portrayal of sex most difficult. In general, these parents perceived this time in their children's lives as their last opportunity to exert some direct influence on their children's development. The playground and peer group pressure encroached increasingly on family time and space and the television was yet another intruder.

The attitude of many parents was one of protectiveness – not just of their child's 'innocence' but also a desire that their children should know enough not to appear silly or misinformed with their peers. Sex had become a reality. It was not just that their children had reached, or were approaching, puberty and so needed to know the facts of life but that their children might be about to become sexually active themselves.

Yet these parents' concern about the depiction of sex was not based solely on a feeling that their children might find out about sex 'too early', and before they were physically or emotionally ready to, but also on a desire not to have to confront their child's sexuality or their child's questions about sex before they, as parents, *had to*. There was still great discomfort with making private issues public. Their children's later bedtime meant that they viewed more television together as a family and this increased the likelihood of their seeing sex scenes. It was also at this age that there was uncertainty about how much the individuals within the family unit knew about each other as sexual beings. Parents and children often felt that they were having to second guess the others' level of knowledge.

> *'Do they know or do they think they have to say something in case I don't know.*
> *They look embarrassed but I'd die if they ever said anything.'*
> *(Daughter, 13, BC1 Family with children, Liverpool)*

For their part children of this age suspected their parents of checking up on them and felt this was an unwanted intrusion upon their independence. They demanded greater freedom in defining what was or was not suitable for them to view. Many families with children of this age had a television in the children's bedroom and this meant that potential battles were often circumvented. A television in the children's bedroom also allowed privacy and an escape from viewing potentially embarrassing programmes as a family. While parents also welcomed this escape, they did express concern that they were abrogating their responsibilities and parental duties too early. There were a number of ways in which these parents achieved a compromise with their children:

(i) They would use the Watershed as the device to move away from a programme. If a programme straddled 9.00 pm, some parents would ask to watch the news on the BBC and switch over (if the child was watching another channel), or they would insist on the child going to bed at the Watershed.

(ii) Some parents would video post-Watershed programmes on the grounds of lateness, rather than explicitly saying they would first vet it. However, if they felt the material was not suitable, many parents would seek to find an excuse not to give the child the video rather than having to tell him or her it was not suitable.

(iii) Some parents said they would suggest another activity in an attempt to draw attention away from the television.

By the time their children reached 16 years of age, parents assumed their children knew most things about sex – and the children presumed that this was what their parents thought.

> *'We've accepted that you are this age and you've got to know these things.'*
> *(Mother, BC1 Family with children 16–19, Thames Valley)*

> *'We already do!'*
> *(Son, 16, BC1 Family with children, Thames Valley)*

Parents often felt that, with children of this age, they were being pulled into a modern way of thinking by their children who insisted 'you shouldn't be so set'. This made parents sometimes feel that they were unwilling participants in the family viewing of scenes which were more explicit than they would have wished, but now they felt they had no control. This sense of reluctant participation was heightened when viewing scenes depicting male or female homosexuality.

> *'It's not the sort of thing you particularly want to see on television (bath scene in*

Making Out*) but if it came on we would see it through ... With our family and the ages they are, you think it's better that these things creep in between our four walls than they go round to someone else's ... Hopefully they make their own adjustments as to how they behave.'*
(Mother, BC1, Family with children 16–19, Thames Valley)

Young people of this age expected that they would be more liberal with their children than their parents were with them, while their parents believed they were more tolerant with their children than their parents had been.

'We as a generation are more broad-minded than our parents, but there's still a couple of steps that we've got to make before we accept that (scene from Journey To Knock*) completely.'*
(Father, BC1 Family with children 16–19, Thames Valley)

'It's the way you said to yourself when you're a kid, "I'm never going to be a mother like her, I'll never do that with my children", but you do end up doing exactly the same.'
(Mother, C2D Family with children under 7, Thames Valley)

Nevertheless, both parents and children of this age felt that, although there were some positive aspects to the coverage of sex-related issues (e.g. AIDS), there were some areas of personal privacy that should never be portrayed (e.g. masturbation).

Respondents claimed that, often when viewing a sex scene as a family, the use of 'distractions' could be desirable and these were frequently found within the programme itself. The devices that alleviated some of the embarrassment were:

(i) If sex was not the main focus of the scene – this was particularly true of comedy where other events might happen at the same time as supposed sexual activity.

An example of this was the excerpt from *Wilt* which respondents were shown. For some respondents the main point of the scene was one character exacting a humiliating revenge on another. For others it was the absurdity of a character tied to an inflatable rubber doll.

(ii) If there was sexual activity implied but no nudity was apparent – many parents felt able to be less explicit in answering their children's questions or in correcting misapprehensions.

'(On scene from Ex*) It's friends cuddling in bed.'*
(Daughter 9, BC1 Family with children 7–11, London)

(iii) If the programme was a comedy – it often made it easier for the viewer to distance himself or herself from the scene and get away from the feeling of being in the bedroom with the characters. Expectations based on one's knowledge of the comic genre allowed one to suspend belief further.

'(Smith and Jones) Doing it in a comedy they're only doing it to get a laugh, it's not serious. If they're doing it in a drama or a film, and it's serious, then you're transported to that place, and you're made to think it's real, you don't think they're actors playing it'.
(Father, C2D Family with children 12–15, London)

(iv) If the characters in the scene did not appear to be enjoying their participation in the action – this was particularly true for the comic genre. (This *excluded* violent sexual scenes). Thus the clip from *Smith and Jones* was more acceptable than was the scene from *The Two of Us*.

'It's different because you can see how much he (Jones) hates it so you sympathize with him. Whereas I don't think you could mime doing that (scene from The Two of Us) *if you weren't enjoying (touching each other).'*
(Mother, C2D Family with children under 7, Thames Valley)

(v) The use of physical distractions – for example the cramp suffered by the female character in *A Journey to Knock*. This was particularly welcome at a point when viewers were becoming uncomfortable about the amount of time the scene of sexual intercourse was taking.

While devices such as those described above helped the family cope with watching a sex scene together, it was inadequate labelling or signing or inappropriate or unexpected material (because of the programme genre, for example) which exacerbated embarrassment. These surprises allowed no time to take any avoiding action, such as choosing not to view as a family.

'Some system that lets you know in advance, that's what's required ... to alert you to strong material ... that would be ideal, because I'm not objecting to it on principle, it's just when it comes on unexpected and there's kids in the room, that's the problem ... the only problem.'
(35–45, male, Slough)

Inappropriate scheduling also raised questions.

'I think when you've got a six year old asking you "What's a condom, mummy?" and you track it down to Neighbours, *you've got to ask what's it doing on at that time.'*
(Social worker, Glasgow)

Parents also expressed other concerns about the inclusion of sexual material in television programmes:

(i) While, as individuals (within the group discussions), they had exhibited a degree of intellectual tolerance about homosexuals and had not agreed that television had any particular influence on children, parents were unhappy about the inclusion of material dealing with homosexuality at a time when their children might be viewing. They expressed concern that such material might trigger a response (that they would consider to be negative) at a stage when their children were uncertain about their own sexuality.

'... you can't help but think that it might trigger them.'
(Mother, BC1 Family with children 12–15, Liverpool)

'I hate it, absolutely hate it. I really hate it. I hate the fact that now people are beginning to accept it as the norm, and the fact that they're showing that (clip from The Two of Us)*in schools ... I know that there are people that are homosexual and lesbian but I hate it.'*
(Mother, C2D Family with children 16–19, Nottingham)

Parents particularly expressed apprehension about their male children. There was a view that girls 'didn't do anything like that' and that, if they did, it was less distasteful and more acceptable.

'That kind of thing (bath scene in Making Out*) is more natural with women anyway. They do touch each other and it's not the same (as it is for males).'*
(Mother, BC1 Family with children 12–15, Liverpool)

(ii) Sexual activity located in a family home was also problematic. The clip from *Brimstone and Treacle* caused alarm (even allowing for the fact that *'you know he's* (Dennis Potter) *always going to be like that').*

'You'd want to make sure you were on your own if you wanted to watch that (Brimstone and Treacle*). Definitely later than 9. More after 10, I'd say'.*
(Father, BC1 Family with children 12–15, Liverpool).

(iii) Another area of concern for parents was the period between the Watershed at 9.00 pm and 10.00 pm. The later time was felt by many parents to be one by which most children might be expected to be in bed and thus they felt it was more appropriate to schedule programmes then which included scenes of sexual activity. Parents argued that the Watershed should be an indication that explicit material might be gradually introduced and not that the 'floodgates' would open.

'I really felt that (rape scene in A Time to Dance*) was over the top. I was just watching it with dada and we both thought it was really abrupt. There just wasn't any warning.'*
(Son, 16, BC1 Family with children 16–19, Thames Valley)

There was an acceptance that there was a difference between those programmes which were explicitly part of children's television (such as *Grange Hill*) and those programmes which were scheduled at a time when children were likely to be watching (such as *EastEnders*). These programmes were recognized as part of 'family viewing' and would be more 'adult' in nature. Nevertheless, parents expected these programmes – broadcast at a time when children could view – to be subject to standards appropriate for the child audience. Thus they did not expect to have to make decisions about the programme's suitability and did not expect to have to monitor transmissions at those times. A number of factors intervened when watching 'family' programmes and these worked in much the same way as the distractions referred to earlier.

(i) If the scene carried on for too long, the tension would often be dissipated by a 'nominated' member of the family.

'We'd probably all sit there and look at it and, in the end, when we're all stuck feeling uncomfortable, dad'll say something, or one of us'll start giggling, or say "oh, I think we've got the message".'
(Son, 16, BC1 Family with children 16–19, Thames Valley)

(ii) The scene's explicitness was an important factor in judging how easy it would be to ignore the issue or disregard the eroticism.

'I mean as long as they've got their clothes on like that (Ex) and they're not actually

showing anything, then there's no problem.. Even if you're watching with young
children, they probably wouldn't understand it anyway and my lot, we could just
ignore it.'
(Mother, BC1 Family with children 12–15, Liverpool)

The avoidance of issues then, was the preferred way in which many parents dealt
with sexual matters. The conflict they felt as individuals when questioned about the
portrayal of sex was largely removed when they answered questions 'as parents'.
They were clearer about the issues and factors which made viewing as a family more
comfortable, and knew the parameters they wished to be set for their children.

3 The acceptability of sexual scenes on television

The previous chapters have shown that there are instances in which scenes depicting sexual activity are, in general, acceptable to the audience. Reference was made to the importance of reducing the element of surprise, and hence possible offence or embarrassment, in such portrayals. The surprise could be caused by a programme that was felt to be inappropriately scheduled, to contain a storyline that did not warrant sexual scenes or to be part of a programme genre in which the depiction of sexual activity was unexpected. This chapter looks more closely at the variables which affect the acceptability of the portrayal of sexual activity on television.

General viewing patterns

A genre of television programming that was felt legitimately to raise issues of a social nature – often as a consequence of a sexual situation – was the soap opera or family serial. This was the most widely viewed genre of programming, with a high loyalty factor.

The most frequently mentioned soap operas were *EastEnders* and *Coronation Street*. The latter was particularly enjoyed by the older and female respondents while the former was most likely to be mentioned by the younger adult audience. *EastEnders* was applauded in particular for addressing important contemporary issues. Indeed some respondents felt that it was complementary to public information broadcasting, 'fleshing out' the consequences of important issues, often related to aspects of sexual activity or sexuality.

> 'Oh, I think serious subjects can be appropriate in soaps...serious issues could be good for my boy, and the characters and events you can identify with. There was a gay in EastEnders ... and AIDS in EastEnders ... and Crossroads had Sandy in a wheelchair which was good ... if it's done properly it can be valuable, subtle.'
> (35–45, male, Slough)

> 'EastEnders has AIDS or HIV and it's educative ... it could change your mind positively because it shows people reacting to a situation. It's not just a statistic. It shows it could happen to anyone. You don't have to be gay or a drugs user. It's

relevant to you.'
(25–35, female, Slough)

Grange Hill was mentioned as an important series for younger people, again because it raised and dealt with social issues. There was some criticism however, about the messages it sometimes conveyed:

'Grange Hill has dealt with drugs and it's put the issue on their level. That's great
... it's a vehicle for getting social issues across.'
(35–45, male, Slough)

'Mind you it showed a girl with a baby having a great time which could be a
dangerous precedent ... And Grange Hill *could encourage them to behave in a*
slovenly way.'
(35–45, male, Slough)

Respondents who were over 55 years of age were less likely to mention the importance of social issues in the programming they saw, possibly because these were of little relevance to them. They did, however, particularly like light entertainment programmes such as quiz shows, and displayed considerable hostility to many (mainly American) films. These were associated, for them, with bad language, offensive and violent attitudes and 'filth'.

'These American films you get now are dirty and revolting ... yes, the ones late at
night have too much sex and bad language and there's no need for it. Now Cagney
and Lacey *are okay.'*
(55+, female, Cambs/Lincs Borders)

Comedy was widely popular but there was considerable variation between the different groups of respondents in the sorts of comedy enjoyed. Younger respondents tended to like 'alternative' comedians. But these were often disliked by the older respondents who felt that they were disrespectful while commenting favourably on comedians such as *Benny Hill* (described by some younger respondents as 'sexist').

'Some of that comedy on Channel 4, that so-called alternative comedy ... it's smutty,
aggressive, it's vicious, sick ... I turn it over ... Now Benny Hill *is light-hearted and*
the girls are nice.'
(55+, male, Bristol)

Homosexual respondents made different demands of comedy. One of them talked of his distaste of the character, Mrs Slocombe, in *Are You Being Served?*

'It's Mrs Slocombe talking about her pussy. I found that horrible. I found that
embarrassing ... it's probably because I'm associating it with a vagina and I find
that offensive you know, even though it's a comedy situation.'
(Gay man[4], Nottingham)

Homosexual respondents argued that homosexual characters were most often introduced in comedy rather than in serious roles, and that they were almost always

---

4 The qualitative research included group discussions and depth interviews with male and female homosexuals. Within the Review it should be noted, therefore, that the term 'homosexual' is used to mean a homosexual of either sex, while the term 'gay man' or 'lesbian' is used to distinguish the gender of the respondent.

stereotyped. This made them feel that they were constantly being reminded of their marginal social status. Characters such as those in *Are You Being Served?* were considered degrading and offensive, serving only to sustain the stereotypes that the heterosexual community had of them.

> *'Kenneth Williams I can find very funny, but I can find it offensive as well – it's the stereotype. It is the handbag scenario they conjure up.'*
> *(Gay man, Nottingham)*

On the other hand, a comedian such as Julian Clary was more acceptable because his sort of humour was considered to be 'gay humour'.

> *'I find Julian Clary hysterical you know. Brilliant. I suppose he's more aware. He shows more awareness of gays. He's not a put-down of gay men.'*
> *(Gay man, Nottingham)*

There is generally little depiction of sex in situation comedies. Drawing on research conducted in the US, Professor Smith (Wolf & Kielwasser, 1991) describes situation comedies as participating 'in that part of real sexuality concerned with taboos – those things which are not supposed to be done or known, those things on the edge of the publicly wholesome at which we peek. For the sitcom, this is a restricted form of the taboo because something as serious as incest, for example, would be beyond the bounds of humour which demarcate the sitcom. In the world of the situation comedy taboo implies the hidden, not the forbidden, so that.. people are frequently discovered saying or doing things they ought not to do by someone else in the family'. Sexual innuendo plays a significant part in situation comedy, as does ironic humour. It plays to the feeling that sexual activity is essentially a private matter.

Sex scenes within serious drama and films, respondents generally agreed, were often a valid device to use. This was only true, however, if they were central to the plot – there was a feeling that they should not be used 'gratuitously'.

> *'There's a difference between sex that is used legitimately in a serious programme where it's natural ... like some Channel 4 play and sex that's sensationalized and nothing to do with the story'.*
> *(20–24, male, Cambs/Lincs Borders)*

> *'(A Time to Dance) It wouldn't have come over the same if they hadn't have shown all them (sexually explicit) parts as well, the obsession with one another, I don't think it would have come across.'*
> *(35–45, female, Manchester)*

As the quantitative results have suggested, many respondents argued that sex was 'natural' and an important part of relationships. As such, it was legitimate for inclusion in a genre such as drama or film which often dealt with aspects of life and relationships. An example given was an explicit sex scene in the play, *The Cloning of Joanna May*. This was accepted on the grounds that it was necessary to demonstrate the obsessive nature of the relationship the principal characters had. As the scene was considered to portray sex in a 'flawed' relationship, this allowed the viewer to distance himself further. Moreover, the play, in itself, resolved the moral and social questions that had been raised by the depiction of sexual activity.

> *'It was showing that he wasn't normal. He still loved his wife, but he was just using*

his girlfriend for sex.'
(Father, BC1 Family with children under 7, Scotland).

Prime variables of acceptability

In addition to defining those broad characteristics which determined the acceptability of a sexual scene within a television programme, the research sought to understand those specific variables which affected the respondent's reaction to the depiction of sexual activity.

This was undertaken, in the quantitative research, first by describing three imaginary scenes in outline, with none of the contextualizing concessions that the audience might normally be expected to make. The scenes progressed from being ambiguous in the visual material seen to being quite explicit. In this way it was felt an initial understanding of the issues surrounding the portrayal of sexual activity could be achieved.[5] Later in the questionnaire respondents were asked to consider possible scenarios on television and radio which dealt more explicity with matters of sexual activity. The results of both these sections are presented below.

> SCENE 1
> 'It is very clear that sex is about to take place, but the couple are not actually shown on the screen while it happens'.

The majority of the sample (87 per cent) found this scene 'very ' or 'quite' acceptable (42 per cent said it was 'very acceptable'). Nearly twice as many respondents aged over 55 said they found it 'not very' or 'not at all' acceptable as the sample as a whole, but they still accounted for less than one in four of that group of older respondents.

The prime reason for the scene's acceptability (see Table 10) was that explicit detail was not shown and so offence would not be taken. Of those who found the scene unacceptable, four per cent said they did so because sex should not be portrayed on television at all.

For each scene, respondents were asked to give their view on the time at which the scene should be transmitted and the time at which they thought it was likely to be shown in the current broadcasting environment. The results are given in Table 11. It should be noted that, for this scene and the others considered, many respondents felt transmission would occur at an earlier time than they themselves thought suitable. Sixty per cent of respondents said that they found 9.00 pm or later the proper time for the transmission of Scene 1, but nearly one-quarter felt that no scheduling restrictions would apply, in fact, to such a scene.

It is also worth noting that 50 per cent of parents with 13–17 year olds were likely to say that 9.00 pm was the better time for the broadcasting of such a scene while one-quarter of 13–24 year olds thought the material was suitable for transmission from 8.00 pm! These results marry well with the qualitative research which had found

---

5   The order in which the scenes were considered was rotated to ensure that ordering effects and biases could be discounted.

that parents of young teenagers, in particular, wished to avoid embarrassing situations when viewing as a family.

Each scene was also examined under a variety of scenarios to understand better the qualitative findings that different programme genres have different boundaries that might apply and that variables such as scheduling or the nature of the relationship portrayed affected a scene's acceptability (see Table 12).

As the qualitative research suggested, sufficient warning and the appropriateness of genre, such as a film, drama series or documentary, were felt to be prime variables which would make this scene acceptable. However, it was still important that such material should be seen to be relevant to the storyline. Other variables such as post-9.00 pm scheduling, the length of the scene, and its setting (i.e. in a bedroom or within an established relationship) were all significant in increasing acceptability. Such material was least acceptable if it was seen to be inappropriate to the genre, was transmitted before the Watershed, occurred in programming obviously viewed by the young (such as pop videos) or if no prior warning was given.

It is worth noting that 81 per cent of those respondents who said that sex scenes on television should be less explicit than they currently are, felt this scene was 'very' or 'quite' acceptable.

Table 10. Scene 1: Reasons for acceptability

Reasons	%
No detail/left to imagination	47
Not offensive	15
OK to show sex on TV	11
OK if in context	8

Table 11. Scene 1: Appropriate transmission times

	Earliest time should be shown %	Would be shown %
Any time	13	24
6–7pm	3	5
7–8pm	7	14
8–9pm	15	19
9–10pm	40	29
10–12am	17	6
12 am+	3	*
Never	3	1

SEX AND SEXUALITY IN BROADCASTING
CORRIGENDA

Page 39: Table 20: Scenario 2
Not very acceptable   21%

Page 43: Table 22: Scenario 4
Not at all acceptable   29%

Page 45: Table 23: Scenario 5
Very acceptable   10%
Quite acceptable   39%
Not very acceptable   33%
Not at all acceptable   17%

Page 87: Paragraph 2 should read
"And because it is not done alone, it is now **NOT** within the
individual's capacity to control entirely".

Page 116: Footnote is incorrectly referenced, and refers to
"<u>Dance of the Seven Veils</u>" in Paragraph 2.

Table 12. Scene 1: Scenarios when acceptable

How acceptable	Very %	Quite %	Not very %	Not at all %
In a programme where a warning has been made beforehand	51	38	7	4
The couple are married	48	40	7	5
In a documentary about sex	50	37	7	6
In a programme shown after 9 pm	46	41	9	4
In a film	41	45	9	6
The scene lasts for a few seconds	37	46	9	7
If it is an important part of the story	37	46	11	6
The couple are in a bedroom	34	48	10	8
In a drama series	30	52	11	7
The woman takes the initiative	22	47	18	12
The man is much older than the woman	19	48	21	12
The couple are having an affair	19	43	25	12
One partner is physically disabled	19	39	20	21
In a soap	15	42	25	18
The scene lasts several minutes	18	38	26	18
In a sit-com	14	40	29	16
In a programme shown before 9 pm	15	26	34	25
The couple are in a place where they can be seen	10	28	37	25
The couple have just met	10	26	36	28
In a programme in which you wouldn't expect to see it	10	26	38	25
In a pop video	10	26	33	31

> SCENE 2
> 'The couple can be seen while sex is taking place but they are covered so no intimate detail is shown'.

While half as many respondents found Scene 2 'very acceptable' as had found Scene 1 acceptable, nearly three quarters of respondents still said that it was 'very' or 'quite' acceptable. Similarly, twice as many respondents said this scene was 'not very acceptable' as had said the same about Scene 1.

The change in acceptability occurred because sexual activity was supposed to be taking place in this scene; in Scene 1 no sexual activity was actually depicted. However, the lack of nudity and explicitness maintained the overall level of acceptability of Scene 2 (Table 13).

While four out of five respondents felt such a scene should only be shown after the Watershed, just over half felt this was actually the case. This echoed the earlier finding that there was a discrepancy between respondents' desired transmission times and their perceptions of the actuality. Nearly one in five respondents said a scene such as Scene 2 would be shown at 8.00 pm while over one-third of the sample said the scene should only be shown after 10.00 pm (Table 14).

As Table 15 shows, the most acceptable genres for such material are, again, films, drama, and documentaries – transmitted, with a warning, post 9.00 pm. Acceptability was enhanced if the relationship portrayed was an established one, while programming easily accessible to young people was felt, in general, not to be a suitable vehicle for a scene such as Scene 2.

Just over half of those respondents who thought sex scenes on television should be less explicit than they are, were likely to say that this was an acceptable scene. This compares with over 80 per cent who had said the same for Scene 1.

Table 13. Scene 2: Reasons for acceptability

Reasons	%
No detail/left to imagination	38
Not offensive	13
OK to show sex on TV	10
Scheduling OK	7
OK if in context	6

Table 14. Scene 2: Appropriate transmission times

	Earliest time should be shown %	Would be shown %
Any time	3	10
6–7pm	1	4
7–8pm	2	11
8–9pm	7	19
9–10pm	50	45
10–12am	26	10
12 am+	3	*
Never	6	1

Table 15. Scene 2: Scenarios when acceptable

How acceptable	Very	Quite	Not very	Not at all
	%	%	%	%
In a programme where a warning has been made beforehand	44	39	9	8
In a documentary about sex	42	39	9	9
The couple are married	37	43	11	9
In a programme shown after 9 pm	36	42	13	8
In a film	33	43	13	10
The scene lasts just a few seconds	30	46	14	10
It's an important part of the story	30	46	14	10
The couple are in a bedroom	28	46	14	11
In a drama series	21	50	17	12
The man is much older than the woman	15	45	23	17
The woman takes the initiative	16	44	23	16
The couple are having an affair	13	43	26	17
One partner is physically disabled	14	35	25	25
The scene lasts several minutes	14	32	31	23
In a sit-com	10	30	34	26
In a soap	10	29	35	26
The couple are in a place where they can be seen	7	23	38	32
The couple have just met	7	21	38	33
In a pop video	6	20	34	40
In a programme in which you wouldn't expect to see it	6	20	39	35
In a programme shown before 9 pm	6	17	37	40

SCENE 3
'Sex is shown in quite explicit detail. The couple are seen naked and very little is left to the imagination'.

As the results of the qualitative research have already indicated, a description such as that for Scene 3 might be expected to lead to a sharp increase in the number of respondents saying such a scene was not acceptable. This was, in fact, true. Now, 34 per cent of respondents said Scene 3 was 'not at all acceptable' in comparison with 10 per cent who had said the same for Scene 2 and 4 per cent who had said this for Scene 1. The greatest increase came in the reaction of those respondents aged over 55; 61 per cent of them now said the televising of such a scene was 'not at all acceptable'. The main reasons cited for the scene's unacceptability were its explicitness and the consequential offensiveness (Table 16).

Most respondents appreciated that scheduling restrictions would apply to such material. However, while nearly two-thirds of respondents thought such a scene should only be shown after 10.00 pm, two in five thought that it would be shown as early as 9.00 pm (Table 17).

It was felt that a film or a documentary were the programme categories most acceptable for the inclusion of such a scene (Table 18). Respondents were concerned that children should not be able to see it and called for scheduling restrictions and a warning. Most respondents felt such a scene would be 'not at all acceptable' in a pop video, for example. Again, the length of time the scene was dwelt upon was important in defining its acceptability as was the relationship being portrayed.

Nearly 90 per cent of those who felt that there should be less explicit sex on television thought that Scene 3 was not acceptable.

In summary then, an analysis of the scenes reiterated the importance of adequate labelling and scheduling restrictions while describing additional variables that could make the depiction of sexual activity admissible to most respondents. These included the suitability of the genre in which the scene took place, the wish that sexual activity should be seen to occur within established relationships and in private, and a concern that such scenes should not be dwelt upon. Other variables such as the physical disability of one partner or the age of the male partner became increasingly important as the scenes became more explicit.

Table 16. Scene 3: Reasons for acceptability

Reasons	%
OK to show sex on TV	11
OK if late	10
If not offensive	8
Always switch off/over	6
Too explicit	16
Offensive	14
Sex shouldn't be on TV	13
Not necessary to story	11
Personal/private matter	8
Not when children around	7

Table 17. Scene 3: Appropriate transmission times

	Earliest time should be shown %	Would be shown %
Any time	1	4
6–7pm	*	1
7–8pm	*	2
8–9pm	1	10
9–10pm	17	41
10–12am	46	28
12 am+	18	7
Never	16	7

Table 18. Scene 3: Scenarios when acceptable

How acceptable	Very %	Quite %	Not very %	Not at all %
In a film	20	39	20	21
In a soap	4	15	31	50
In a documentary about sex	31	41	11	16
In a programme shown before 9 pm	2	5	20	72
In a programme shown after 9 pm	19	38	24	19
In a sit-com	4	16	30	50
In a pop video	2	10	24	65
In a programme in which you wouldn't expect to see it	3	13	29	55
In a drama series	11	37	26	25
In a programme where a warning annoucement has been made	33	39	12	16
The couple are married	25	37	17	20
The couple are having an affair	11	32	28	29
The couple are in a bedroom	18	40	20	22
The couple are in a place where they may be seen	5	15	32	48
The couple have just met	5	16	31	48
It's an important part of the story	19	41	19	21
The man is older than the woman	10	37	26	27
The woman takes the initiative	11	37	25	27
The scene lasts just a few seconds	19	42	18	21
The scene lasts several minutes	8	25	28	38
One partner is physically disabled	7	29	25	38

Imaginary scenarios

While the scenes outlined above were used to understand the main variables that mattered such as scheduling and programme genre, six individual scenarios were used to investigate in greater detail, and in more realistic contexts, how respondents would react to certain events on television, and to understand how parameters such as context affected the acceptability of a scene depicting sexual activity.[6]

SCENARIO 1

The first scenario was described to the respondent as:

> A scene from the dramatized version of a novel by a well-known and respected author, shown late in the evening. One of the female characters is having an affair with a friend she has known for a long time. They peel each other's clothes off in front of the living room fire, then he lies on the sofa and she climbs on top of him to have sex. The camera remains fixed on them as they achieve a mutual climax.

---

6   For reasons of interview time and cost, the sample was split so that each respondent was only ever required to consider three scenarios.

Over one-half of respondents (57 per cent) felt that such material was not acceptable (61 per cent of the over 55 year olds said it was 'not at all acceptable' in comparison with 30 per cent of the sample in general). Another third (35 per cent) that it was 'quite acceptable' and 7 per cent said it was 'very acceptable' (Table 19).

As we noted when examining the factors that increased the acceptability of the various scenes outlined earlier, variables such as the scheduling of the programme were of great importance. Nearly three-quarters of respondents to this scenario said that its late placing made it acceptable. Also of importance were the fact that the scene occurred in an adaptation of a novel by an author who was both well-known and respected and that it was one scene in the entire programme. Many respondents felt the fact that the camera remained on the characters as they were depicted making love or that the supposed sexual act continued until a climax was reached made the scene less acceptable. Based on our knowledge of the qualitative findings, one might expect that this level of explicitness could create embarrassment.

Respondents were asked if other people might want to see such a programme, and were then probed for their judgement on the showing of such material. Over half the sample thought that people would want to see a scenario such as this but respondents were divided as to whether or not it should be shown. (It is worth noting that 76 per cent of respondents aged over 55 said that they did not think such material should be shown at all.)

Respondents were also asked if they thought there were any specific controls that should be applied to the transmission of a scene such as this – over one-third mentioned the importance of a warning and a further 36 per cent mentioned the importance of late scheduling. As the group discussions and other interviews had found, many respondents would prefer to be able to take avoiding action rather than risk embarrassment or offence or, indeed, call for a ban on the transmission of a programme. Over one half of respondents (56 per cent) said that they had seen a similar scene on television.

Respondents were probed for their likely responses if they were to see such a scene when watching alone or when they were watching with the person they most often viewed television with. They were also asked to guess that other person's reactions to the scenario.

As one might have been led to expect from the qualitative research, respondents were more likely to accept Scenario 1 if they were watching television alone. Twice as many respondents claimed that they would feel embarrassed watching such material with someone else than if they were viewing on their own. They also believed that the other person would be embarrassed.

Table 19. Scenario 1: Acceptability

Very acceptable %	Quite acceptable %	Not very acceptable %	Not at all acceptable %
7	35	27	30

	%
Reasons for acceptability:	%
It is shown late in the evening	74
It's one scene in an episode	37
It's from a novel	34
It's written by a respected author	26
The couple are friends of many years	25
It's written by a well-known author	20
The couple are having an affair	17
The camera remains fixed on them	12
The climax is mutual	12
The woman is on top of the man	11
They lie on the sofa	10

	%
Reasons for unacceptability:	%
The camera remains fixed on them	71
You see them achieve a climax	58
The climax is mutual	42
The woman is on top of the man	35
They take their clothes off	31
The couple are having an affair	17
They lie on the sofa	14
They're in the living room	10

	%
Would other people want to see it?	%
Yes	56
No	24
Don't know	20

	%
Should it be on?	%
Yes	51
No	43
Don't know	6

	%
If no, should it be banned?	%
Yes	48
No	44
Don't know	8

Scenario 1: The viewing context

	How you feel when watching alone	How you feel when watching with someone else	What you think they feel
	%	%	%
It's OK if it's part of the story	34	26	21
It could happen	31	21	17
There's nothing wrong with showing that	29	26	27
I'll switch off/over	28	27	27
I was surprised	27	17	15
This is too explicit	23	20	14
It's erotic	19	13	14
How embarrassing	15	32	27
It's only make-believe	15	12	12
It's tastefully done	14	9	8
It's disgusting	14	12	12
It's really offensive	14	11	10
It's romantic	11	11	9

SCENARIO 2

The second imagined scenario was:

> An episode of an historical drama shown late in the evening. Set in Ancient Rome, it is based on a true story. During the programme there is a scene in a brothel, where lots of wine, women and song result in a full-scale orgy. Characters are seen swopping partners, in unconventional sexual positions and having sex with more than one person at a time. Although there are a range of characters involved, most are overweight, wealthy Romans, whilst the prostitutes are all young and beautiful.

This scenario was not thought to be very acceptable with only six per cent of the sample saying that it was. Slightly more respondents were likely to say that this scenario was 'not at all acceptable' in comparison with those saying the same for Scenario 1.

When probed for the particular variables that make it more, or less, acceptable, respondents were inclined to say that the scene's late transmission time and its foundation in a true story, with an appropriate backdrop, were important. However, the unconventionality of the setting also increased its unacceptability – respondents did not like the fact that the scene was set in an orgy with characters involved with multiple partners and a variety of sexual positions being depicted.

Despite this, over 60 per cent of respondents thought that other people might want to see such a scene and one-half thought that it should be on for those that wished to see it (Table 20). Most respondents (71 per cent) did not think, however, that they had ever seen such a scene.

Again, over one-third of respondents said that adequate warning beforehand and appropriate scheduling were important and justified controls for such material.

When probed about the context in which they might see such a scenario, more respondents were likely to say that they would switch the television off if they happened to see such a scene than had said the same for Scenario 1. In fact, they were more inclined to say they would take this action if they were watching on their own and many respondents commented on the increase in embarrassment they, and their viewing partners, would feel if such a scene came on.

Table 20. Scenario 2: Acceptability

Very acceptable %	Quite acceptable %	Not very acceptable %	Not at all acceptable %
6	35	27	38

	%
Reasons for acceptability:	%
It's shown late in the evening	73
It's based on a true story	70
It's an historical drama	58
It's set in Ancient Rome	49
It's one episode in a series	32
The scene is in a brothel	24
They drink lots of wine	15
They're prostitutes	13
They're overweight Romans	11
They're wealthy Romans	10
They're young and beautiful prostitutes	10
There's a full scale orgy	10
Reasons for unacceptability:	%
They have sex with more than one person at a time	78
They're swapping partners	70
There's a full scale orgy	66
They're in unconventional sexual positions	65
The scene is in a brothel	33
They're prostitutes	28
They're young and beautiful prostitutes	20
They drink lots of wine	12
They're overweight Romans	10
Would other people want to see it?	%
Yes	61
No	25
Don't know	14

Should it be on?	%
Yes	50
No	46
Don't know	3

If no, should it be banned?	%
Yes	58
No	35
Don't know	7

Scenario 2: The viewing context

	How you feel when watching alone	How you feel when watching with someone else	What you think they feel
	%	%	%
I'll switch off/over	40	33	32
I was surprised	28	17	16
It's OK if it's part of the story	28	22	18
This is too explicit	25	22	20
It's really offensive	24	19	16
It's disgusting	23	19	19
There's nothing wrong with showing that	22	22	24
It could happen	19	13	11
I can't relate to it	18	15	12
It's erotic	18	15	13
How embarrassing	14	32	26
It's only make-believe	13	11	10

SCENARIO 3

The third scenario, a dramatized documentary on television, was described thus:

> A scene in a dramatized documentary about a boys' school, shown in the late evening. A young boy is in the showers alone, having been kept behind for a detention for misbehaving in class. An older boy comes in to the shower, sees the younger boy and decides to take advantage of the situation. He slowly corners the frightened boy, talking reassuringly to him as he starts to kiss and caress him. His embrace becomes stronger as the scene fades. The next scene shows the smaller boy crying on his bed.

Despite the fact that this was a documentary, it was felt to be considerably less acceptable than the two scenarios thus far considered (Table 21).

The reasons for the strong rejection of this scenario all hinged on the fact that the younger boy was seduced, against his will, by the older boy and the respondents' dislike of the fact that the older boy was able to take advantage of him. The redeeming features of this scenario were the fact that it was a documentary and transmitted late at night. The depiction of physical contact between the boys also decreased the scenario's acceptability.

The strength of feeling against this scenario was further underlined in consideration of the results to the other questions about it. Three out of five respondents did not believe other people would want to see such a scenario and an even greater number said it should not be on. Three-quarters of those who said they did not think it should be transmitted went on to say that they would ban such a scene. Issues such as appropriate scheduling and prior warning were only of relevance to about a quarter of the respondents.

Seven out of ten respondents felt that they had not seen anything of this sort on television before. Again, they were asked about their reactions *should* they see such a scene, when watching alone and when viewing with their regular partner, and that person's probable response.

As the strong negative responses noted above might suggest, nearly half of all respondents questioned about this scenario said that they would switch off the television or change channels, regardless of whether or not they were watching with someone else. Interestingly, and in contrast to the other scenarios considered, most respondents claimed that they would be more offended and would find the scene more disgusting if they were watching on their own. It is possible that the fact that the scene was set within a documentary made it more acceptable for joint viewing. If the scene had been a drama the reaction may well have been in a similar vein to that for the other scenarios – that is, greater embarrassment would have been experienced when viewing with someone else.

Table 21. Scenario 3: Acceptability

Very acceptable %	Quite acceptable %	Not very acceptable %	Not at all acceptable %
2	15	26	57

	%
Reasons for acceptability:	%
It's a documentary	64
It's shown late in the evening	60
It's just one scene	24
The small boy is crying/upset	16
The young boy is cornered/frightened	12
The older boy takes advantage	10

Reasons for unacceptability:	%
The older boy takes advantage	64
It involves a young boy	62
The young boy is cornered/frightened	58
There are two boys kissing	53
There are two boys caressing	52
The small boy is crying/upset	49
It's set in a boy's school	14
It's set in a shower	13
The young boy has been kept behind/in detention	11

Would other people want to see it?	%
Yes	25
No	61
Don't know	14

Should it be on?	%
Yes	25
No	71
Don't know	3

If no, should it be banned?	%
Yes	74
No	21
Don't know	4

Scenario 3: The viewing context

	How you feel when watching alone	How you feel when watching with someone else	What you think they feel
	%	%	%
I'll switch off/over	47	49	45
It's disgusting	40	34	36
It's really offensive	36	28	23
It could happen	28	22	17
This is too explicit	24	20	18
I was surprised	22	17	16
I can't relate to it	20	16	11
How embarrassing	15	20	24
It's OK if it's part of the story	10	13	11

SCENARIO 4

The fourth scenario was:

> A scene from an early evening soap opera. One of the main female characters is committing adultery with the next door neighbour. She is a very glamorous forty year old, but he has only just left school. They go into the bedroom in a passionate embrace, and the door closes on them. They are next seen lying in bed after having sex.

Nearly two in five respondents thought this was an acceptable scene to be shown. Those aged over 55 years were significantly more likely to say that it was 'not at all acceptable' in comparison with the sample as a whole (54 per cent of those aged 55+ said this versus 29 per cent of the total sample).

The reasons for the scenario's acceptability were the fact that it was only one scene and was not over-explicit. Some respondents found it unacceptable because of the time at which it was scheduled (early evening), that the couple were 'seen' in bed after sex, that it was an episode from a soap opera and that the woman was committing adultery with a much younger man.

The majority of respondents agreed that other people would want to see such a scene but two in five thought that it should not be on. About one-third of all respondents went on to say that appropriate scheduling would be an acceptable control to put on the showing of such material.

Despite the fact that 40 per cent of the sample said such a scene should not be transmitted, about one-half of respondents thought that they had seen something similar and, in general, displayed less extreme reactions to the possibility of viewing such a scenario than they had to the others. Once again, however, respondents' claimed level of embarrassment doubled if they thought that they might see such a scene in the company of someone else.

Table 22. Scenario 4: Acceptability

Very acceptable %	Quite acceptable %	Not very acceptable %	Not at all acceptable %
7	31	32	39

Reasons for acceptability:	%
It's just one scene	53
The bedroom door closes on them	52
It's a soap opera	35
They're seen in bed after having sex	30
The woman is glamorous	17
They go into the bedroom	15

43

Reasons for unacceptability:	%
It's shown in the early evening	62
They're seen in bed after having sex	45
It's a soap opera	42
The woman is committing adultery	40
The man's younger/he's just left school	40
They embrace passionately	18
They go into the bedroom	16
The woman is 40 years old	15
She's with her next door neighbour	14
The bedroom door closes on them	12

Would other people want to see it?	%
Yes	55
No	28
Don't know	16

Should it be on?	%
Yes	51
No	42
Don't know	7

If no, should it be banned?	%
Yes	51
No	37
Don't know	12

Scenario 4: The viewing context

	How you feel when watching alone	How you feel when watching with someone else	What you think they feel
	%	%	%
It could happen	39	24	22
It's OK if it's part of the story	30	22	21
There's nothing wrong with showing that	29	24	25
I'll switch off/over	22	23	19
I was surprised	21	15	13
It's only make believe	20	15	14
It's disgusting	14	9	10
I can't relate to it	14	6	9
It's tastefully done	13	9	7
How embarrassing	9	16	16

SCENARIO 5

The fifth scenario also considered an early evening programme, but this one was a drama.

> A scene from an early evening drama series. A newly married couple are about to make love for the first time since the wedding. They can be partly seen in the low, romantic lighting as they slowly undress and have sex. Soft music is playing in the background and sounds of pleasure can be heard.

Except to the over 55 year olds, this was the most acceptable of the fictional scenarios considered.

The reasons for its acceptability were that it was not explicit, that the couple portrayed were newly married and the scene was only one in an entire drama. The reasons that some respondents found it unacceptable were the time of transmission (early evening), the fact that the couple were having sex at all and that one could hear them.

Nearly three-quarters of all respondents thought that other people might want to see such material, and about the same number thought that it should be on. Indeed, over three out of five respondents thought that they already *had* seen such a scene on television.

Nevertheless, embarrassment when viewing with one's normal viewing partner was expressed. Respondents not only said that they would become embarrassed but more said they would switch channels and they were less likely to make excuses for the scene, such as there was 'nothing wrong' or that it was 'romantic', in comparison with comments for the other scenarios.

Table 23. Scenario 5: Acceptability

Very acceptable %	Quite acceptable %	Not very acceptable %	Not at all acceptable %
7	31	32	39

Reasons for acceptability:	%
They're only partly seen	61
They're newly married	60
It's just one scene	45
It's a drama series	39
They're about to make love for the first time since the wedding	33
There's low romantic lighting	31
There's soft background music	23
They're about to make love	16
You hear sounds of pleasure	10

	%
Reasons for unacceptability:	
It's shown in the early evening	71
They have sex	50
You hear sounds of pleasure	48
They're about to make love	29
They undress slowly	23
They're about to make love for the first time since the wedding	16
They're a newly married couple	10

	%
Would other people want to see it?	
Yes	72
No	14
Don't know	14

	%
Should it be on?	
Yes	73
No	22
Don't know	5

	%
If no, should it be banned?	
Yes	41
No	47
Don't know	13

Scenario 5: The viewing context

	How you feel when watching alone	How you feel when watching with someone else	What you think they feel
	%	%	%
There's nothing wrong with that	40	30	29
It's OK if it's part of the story	39	25	6
It could happen	35	23	21
It's romantic	33	20	17
It's tastefully done	24	15	2
I'll switch off/over	17	23	18
It's only make believe	17	13	13
I was surprised	15	11	4
How embarrassing	8	20	19

SCENARIO 6

The sixth, and final, scenario considered a radio documentary on child abuse.

A radio documentary in the early evening about child abuse. The physical and emotional effects on the child are discussed in detail, and a lively discussion follows amongst social workers, doctors and programme makers.

Unlike Scenario 3, a dramatized documentary, over 70 per cent of respondents thought this scenario, also a documentary, was 'very' or 'quite' acceptable (Table 24).

The overwhelming reasons for its acceptability were that it was factual with participants drawn from the professions that would be involved in a case of child abuse. Some respondents found it unacceptable because of the level of detail that was entered into, particularly physical details, and the timing of transmission.

The majority of respondents also said that they thought other people would be interested in such a programme and felt that it should be on. One-third of respondents said that if people did not want to hear it, they should switch off the radio. It was generally felt to be an important topic, warranting serious consideration. Appropriate controls on scheduling and the importance of a prior warning were also mentioned as desirable by about one-quarter of respondents.

Three-quarters of the respondents thought that they had not heard such a programme on the radio before and, while they felt it was a good and important subject for the radio to cover, they would prefer to listen to it on their own.

Table 24. Scenario 6: Acceptability

Very acceptable %	Quite acceptable %	Not very acceptable %	Not at all acceptable %
24	48	17	11

Reasons for acceptability:	%
It's a documentary	75
Doctors are involved	60
A discussion follows	59
Social workers are involved	53
It's about child abuse	50
Emotional effects are discussed	45
It's on the radio	42
Physical effects are discussed	37
The programme makers are involved	28
The emotional effects are discussed in detail	20
The physical effects are discussed in detail	17

Reasons for unacceptability:	%
The physical effects are discussed in detail	69
It's on in the early evening	54
The emotional effects are discussed in detail	53
It's about child abuse	45
Physical effects are discussed	42
Emotional effects are discussed	33
A discussion follows	17
The programme makers are involved	16
Social workers are involved	13
It's on the radio	10

Would other people want to see it?	%
Yes	80
No	12
Don't know	8

Should it be on?	%
Yes	87
No	9
Don't know	5

If no, should it be banned?	%
Yes	39
No	36
Don't know	15

Scenario 6: The viewing context

	How you feel when watching alone	How you feel when watching with someone else	What you think they feel
	%	%	%
It's good to talk about these things	59	51	36
It could happen	52	40	30
It's interesting	31	28	29
It's tastefully done	18	5	3
I'll switch off/over	16	21	25
This could encourage more child abuse	16	17	16
I can't relate to it	11	6	10

The scenarios developed the findings, derived from an analysis of the scenes, that the parameters of scheduling and programme genre were particularly important in any consideration of the portrayal of sexual activity. The significance of context and the placing of the episode were all marked as important factors in increasing acceptability. The scenarios also showed, however, that none of the variables on its own necessarily offered a legitimate vehicle for the depiction of sexual activity. For example, one might have supposed that the documentary described in Scenario 3, which showed little such material and was a programme genre in which it seemed to be generally admissible to portray sexual activity, would be acceptable. This was not the case. It would seem that the dramatization, and inclusion of physical contact between the two young men, created doubts in the minds of respondents. It may be that the description could not offer a valid reason for the inclusion of such a recon-struction – it is more likely that the portrayal of sexual activity between males, particularly when one partner was seen to be vulnerable, would not have been acceptable in any circumstance. In contrast, the factual documentary described in Scenario 6, while dealing with a sensitive issue, was the most acceptable of the scenarios. The importance of the media used should also be mentioned. Scenario 6 occurred on the radio, possibly allowing the respondent greater privacy, and thereby reducing the potential embarrassment of being part of a larger audience.

Rules in programming

In summary, despite the greater 'lenience' afforded certain categories of programm-ing, the Council's research found that respondents believed there were still rules to be observed.

> (i) Sex scenes should be 'meaningful' and not gratuitous. A sex scene had to be justified first by the genre of programming in which it occurred. There was a strong feeling expressed about the 'appropriateness' of categories – a drama often dealt with human inter-relationships in which sex might form a natural part, while a sex scene in a detective series was felt to be quite inappropriate. The purpose of that latter type of programme, it was felt, was to unravel a mystery and not to explore personal relationships.

> *'You sort of know in a play or something, later at night, sex is liable to come into it, and that's okay because it's about real relationships ... but in some detective thing that's really just a who-done-it, it wouldn't seem right at all.'*
> *(35–45, male, Slough)*

> The dramatic or narrative context of the episode or scene in which sex arose was also important and there was concern expressed about the use of sex to 'shock'.

> It was felt also that sexual activity should occur within meaningful relation-ships thus acting as a role model for younger viewers. The portrayal of a 'one-night-stand' was felt to be less easy to justify and women, in particular, felt strongly about this.

> *'It's okay if it's in context in a relationship, not just quick sex between strangers, that could send out the wrong signals.'*

> *'(Another) Especially with AIDS.'*
> *(20–24, females, Harrow)*

> *'When they just jump into bed within 24 hours and you never see any courtship ...*

49

now that could have a negative influence on kids ... they begin to think that sort of thing is normal.'
(35–45, male, Slough)

(ii) The programme containing the scene should be adequately labelled or signed:

'(Brimstone and Treacle clip) That should be on late on Channel 4 ... 11.00 pm ... they could do more to show it's that type of programme, a special sign beside the title, that way you can always turn off if you want.'
(30–45, male, Sheffield)

Respondents also felt that warnings were an important and useful tool in allowing them to avoid material which could offend or embarrass. There was a strong feeling that the more information a viewer had in order to make a decision about viewing a particular programme, coupled with the knowledge of who she/he would be viewing with, the less legitimate it was to complain.

'I don't know why there was so much fuss about (the sex in) that Time to Dance, *it was in all the newspapers, you know what it's going to be like'.*
(Mother, BC1 Family with children under 7, Scotland)

(iii) Programmes which included sex scenes should obey scheduling restrictions (defined often by the Watershed at 9.00 pm). This was felt to be particularly important as the conventions of the Watershed were well known. Respondents felt that it could be used to avoid embarrassment, particularly if one was viewing with other family members before whom one might feel discomfort.

Despite the recognition of the customs of the Watershed, there was a feeling that it could be improved. It was generally agreed that it was acceptable to address issues related to sex in the early evening soap operas which were targeted at a family audience but often watched by children. It was not legitimate to include actual depictions of sexual activity until children were considered to be in bed. Many respondents questioned the 9.00 pm Watershed as being too early for older children, with whom viewing would be an embarrassment, and some respondents thought that 10.00 pm was a better time for the depiction of sex.

'9 o'clock is too early a Watershed, it should be 10.00 because the young kids are up later now'.
(55+, male, Bristol)

'But there's the issue of when it (sexually explicit material) should be shown. There are lots of impressionable young kids with a TV in their bedroom ... after 10.00 is okay, when it's your 15 to 16 year olds watching.'

'(Another) Yes, after 10.00 it's the people's choice.'
(20–24, males, Cambs/Lincs. Borders)

'I think with the changing times, kiddies do tend to stay up later and all of a sudden they are watching kiddies' programmes and then it's 9 o'clock and that's it, x rated stuff. Well, you have to be 18 to see that sort of thing in the pictures you know and yet why should you say to a 11 or 12 year old child "right that's it, well sorry it's

bedtime, you are not allowed to see the telly".'
(35–45, female, Manchester)

There were some respondents in the group discussions, all men, who felt that 'soft porn' (defined as 'sex-for-its-own-sake' programming) or other minority interest programming should be sanctioned, but these, they felt, should be restricted to transmission outside main viewing hours.

'At 16 you can have sex. At 17 you can be in the army and kill people, but you need to be 18 to see a Blue Movie! ... so after 10.00 pm why can't there be pornography ... the sort with sex and a story, but not deviance.'
(20–24, male, Cambs/Lincs Borders)

Many female respondents did not feel able to condone the showing of 'soft porn' at any time, and argued that men could rent similar material on video if they wished.

'Pornography serves a purpose. Men get turned on by physical sex ... they could put porn on late at night.'

'(Another) But it could be a wind-up, it could encourage rape.'

'... personally I don't want to see it. It challenges the way I want to see sex.'
(25–35, females, Slough)

Women held the view, about themselves, that they would only want to see the portrayal of sexual activity in relationships. However, when they were questioned further, some women said that they might be interested in seeing some sexual programming.

'(Moderator: so what about showing blue films after midnight?) Well, I wouldn't mind.' (Another) 'No, me neither.'

'(Another) I'd maybe watch it. It wouldn't be so bad after a drink though I wouldn't plan to watch it.'
(18–19, females, Sheffield)

Despite many respondents' agreement that programming for groups such as homosexuals should be available, they were torn between a recognition that they should be tolerant of homosexuality and the personal aversion many of them claimed to feel towards the idea of homosexuality. Broadcasting material for homosexuals outside the main viewing hours would help to ease the tensions felt.

'(Sebastiane) It's not something I'd watch. It's unpleasant, it would make me turn off 'cause it doesn't do anything for me ... but I wouldn't censor it. Some blokes who are that way inclined will probably like it and for them it's okay to broadcast it ... I'd say they could put that stuff on, when it's minority audience time.'
(30–45, male, Sheffield)

(iv) As the scenes and scenarios showed, there were clear rules to be followed about the sort of sexual activity that could be shown. Respondents had a clear idea of how far television should go in terms of depicting the sexual act and the level of detail that was acceptable. Respondents accepted that these expectations were based on their own personal standards and conditioning.

51

They expected to see female nudity and some male nudity, but they did not expect to see a full male frontal. Mention was made, however, of *A Time To Dance* in which the principal male character was briefly seen naked, and this was recognized as a breakthrough.

'Yes it seems to be moving to more openness...there are things on now you'd never have had ten years back ... I don't know about it, but I suppose it's okay, because it's not healthy to brush it under the carpet like in our parents' day, but it could go too far.'
(30–45, female, Harrow)

Respondents expected to see characters caressing, to hear heavy breathing and to see writhing (principally under sheets) which would suggest copulation. They did not expect to see a variety of positions for intercourse, close ups of genitalia, penetration, oral sex, group sex or homosexual activity (male or female).

'Normally you just see the tops of their bodies when they're supposed to be at it, you don't see their whole bodies when they're at it.'
(30–45, male, Sheffield)

'They never show anything other than the basic act ... no funny positions or her sucking him off or anything like that.'
(20–24, male, Cambs/Lincs. Borders)

'Oh I'm sure in ten years I'm sure they probably will ... you'll see male erections on the screen and it will be normal.'
(30–45, female, Harrow)

Respondents in the quantitative study were asked who they usually watched television with. In the early evening nearly half of all respondents said they watched with their partners. Just over 40 per cent of parents said that they watched with their children. During the evening however, the proportion of those viewing with children or relatives other than their partner decreased. Slightly more respondents (over half of the sample) said they viewed with their partners in the late evening, while only about 10 per cent of parents said they were watching television with their children at that time.

Radio listening was a more solitary occupation – 36 per cent of the respondents who said they listened to the radio claimed to listen alone in the early evening. Just over one in ten said they listened with their partner.

As has already been mentioned, respondents were torn between feelings of personal discomfort and a recognized need for tolerance in most areas concerning sex. They were uncertain whether or not material should be censored or banned, thereby preventing others from viewing it.

With an understanding of the parameters that affect the sensitivities of the audience, particularly in relation to the portrayal of sex, the broadcaster is able to avoid causing offence and is better able to allow the viewer or listener to take action to evade embarrassment.

4 The special concerns of the homosexual

In general the research found that the homosexual respondents interviewed found it difficult to demand that anything be prohibited from television because they felt so marginalized by society (see essay by Dr Morrison). However many of them did object to programming which showed the subjugation of one person by another. They insisted that people should not be seen only as sex objects on television. This was particularly true of the lesbian respondents, although all the homosexuals talked about their desire for equality of characterization on television.

> 'You don't see plays about 45 year old women picking up 20 year old toyboys. You know, you just don't see it ... she is a bimbo, she is a sex object. You know, good for a bang. Our relationships are more equal'.
> (Lesbian, Nottingham)

Just as some parents and heterosexuals had expressed distaste about watching homosexual sex, so some homosexuals expressed revulsion at watching the representation of heterosexual sex – although they realized that they could not, and should not, call for it to be censored.

> 'It strikes me that most of the straight sex on the telly is a bit wham bang.'
> (Gay man, London)

So, while not believing in censorship per se there was a feeling that perhaps certain material should not be shown, but this related far more to the portrayal of violence than of sex.

> 'I feel children and young people grow up with adults sort of saying no sex, no violence and it's all grouped together. To me, I object to violence on the telly. I would say a lot of that should be on much later, but the sex stuff, no.'
> (Lesbian, London)

Despite this, many of the homosexual respondents realized that this might be difficult for some parents and they were concerned that children should be offered guidance when watching programmes which included homosexuals or programmes depicting homosexual relationships.

> *'I think with a lot of stuff it is important with children to actually be with them, to watch it maybe, and answer questions in a positive way.'*
> (lesbian, London)

Research conducted in 1988 by Docherty, Morrison and Tracey had found that male homosexual respondents were, at that time, appreciative of the contribution that Channel Four had made to programming aimed at them. But it also found mixed reactions – some respondents had felt that they did not want attention drawn to themselves while others complained of being 'ghettoized' into late-night slots. The type of programming being demanded by these two groups differed – the first group wanted programming in which homosexuals were accepted as a fact of society and in which the sexuality of the characters was incidental. The second group wanted homosexual 'entertainment'. The results from the interviews conducted with homosexuals for this Review would suggest that the former is still called for, and perhaps by most homosexuals, while some part of the wishes of the latter group have been met.

The homosexual respondents were more interested in the way in which sexuality was 'packaged' by television rather than by the way in which the sexual act was portrayed. They felt it important that homosexuality was presented in the same way as heterosexuality and that the characters who were homosexuals were seen not only in stereotypical roles (as in comedy). They stressed that television programming should show that homosexuals were people who had particular sexual preferences. Through such characterizations, they felt they could remove their defensive stance in society and be more honest about their feelings and sexuality.

> *'I think it is good to have programmes like we have been having on Channel 4 and BBC 2 but I mean I think it also would be a good thing to have gay and lesbian characters in any sorts of programmes so that we are not seen as something very special ... Just as part of the furniture you know, no different.'*
> (Gay man, Nottingham)

Many of the respondents had not been able to admit their sexuality to their families and they felt that the legitimization of homosexuality, through its portrayal on television, might help their own lives. When hypothesizing on viewing the clip from *Two of Us* with their families, one respondent said:

> *'My father wouldn't say anything. He would run out of the room or cover his eyes and say arrgh! and run because he is so homophobic.'*
> (Gay man, London)

The homosexual respondents suggested that characters within programmes should be allowed to be established before their sexuality becomes apparent. This would allow sympathy for a character to form before his or her sexuality became an issue. An example given was:

> *'Someone like 'a well established character' in* EastEnders *that has actually been in it for a long time and then all of a sudden there is a growing awareness that she is a lesbian.'*
> (Lesbian, Nottingham)

> *'I am fed up actually with homosexuals being on television just to address the issue*

of homosexuality ... there are no homosexual doctors who are there because they have a doctor in the story.'
(Gay man, London)

At the time of research, BBC2 had recently shown the play *The Lost Language of Cranes*. This dealt with a young man's decision to reveal his homosexuality to his parents and the subsequent disclosure that the father was homosexual. It showed scenes of homosexual lovemaking as well as depicting the social environment of some homosexuals. The recency of the transmission meant the researcher was able to question homosexual respondents about the play and explore their attitudes and opinions to it.

In general respondents welcomed the play, feeling it was a fair portrayal of homosexuality, showing an 'average relationship' between a young man and his lover (although some respondents criticized it for being too 'arty').

'I enjoyed it because of its positive stereotyping. The women in the programme got a bad deal out of what was happening because of the homosexual relationship. I didn't enjoy that too much, but I did enjoy the portrayal of a homosexual relationship.'
(Gay man, London)

'The Cranes had something I could actually identify with and get involved with.'
(Gay man, London)

A further criticism of the play was that, although it did portray a homosexual relationship in a constructive way, it did not show the possible normalcy of a homosexual couple. It did not show, for example, that a homosexual relationship could be a long-term one in the same way as a heterosexual relationship might be.

Many of the homosexual respondents said that the play held back in its depiction of sexual activity and was constrained by the wider audience which would include non-homosexual viewers. As a result, one saw a lot less sex than one might have done if it had been a play about heterosexuals.

'I think it left a lot to the imagination like some of the heterosexual scenes that we would have had on the telly perhaps a few years ago.'
(Gay man, London)

When asked about the possible response that a heterosexual audience might have had to the play, homosexual respondents offered no view, and saw the play completely from their individual sexual perspectives, in much the way that many of the heterosexual respondents had viewed the portrayal of homosexuality.

Television was seen as hostile in the main because it served to deny, by omission and commission, the identity of homosexuals. The model of sexuality that was constantly being presented was of heterosexuality. Lesbians believed that they were treated less well than gay men by television – their sexual preferences were either ignored or included for titillation. With reference to *The Lost Language of Cranes*:

'I think it is terrible that they portrayed the male side of it but not the female side ... the woman who is writing a thesis, she is a lesbian and in the book it was a heavy story.'
(Lesbian, London)

And to excite ...

> *'I think sex between two men is less acceptable than sex between two women ... It's (lesbian scenes) very titillating to men whereas to the heterosexual male two men is usually viewed as disgusting, terrible.'*
> *(Lesbian, London)*

Indeed when the general group discussions were conducted, a thread of this could be seen to be running through respondents' responses. Greater tolerance was displayed towards lesbianism:

> *'Lesbianism is more acceptable (than male homosexuality) because they are an attractive sex to watch ... and women are loving, soft, naturally affectionate ... but (male) homosexuality is out.'*
> *(35–45, male, Slough)*

Non-homosexual respondents imagined lesbian sex to be passive, not penetrative or physically damaging. Some respondents said they felt that women might 'fall into' a lesbian relationship because of maltreatment from a male partner. Male homosexuals, on the other hand, were felt to be more pro-active and therefore more in charge of their homosexual status.

This created conflict because men were required to be seen as strong, resilient, not overly emotional or affectionate towards each other. When male respondents were confronted with this male stereotype and questioned about its desirability, some expressed their doubts.

> *'Men are supposed to be men, not effeminate. They should be tough emotionally, they're not supposed to show their tears ... Now that's not necessarily a good thing but generally you'll find it's the tough guy who comes out as the leader.'*
> *(55+, male, Bristol)*

> *'I think male homosexuality opposes the values of ordinary men ... (Sebastiane clip shown) ... oh, that's not how I see a man ... are these actors queer? ... the mouth to mouth, I'm not sure about that ... it's not the way we see men ... you think of men being a bit macho on the outside. It's only in a relationship you see the softer side.'*
> *(20–24, female, Harrow).*

Attitudes to the portrayal of homosexuality

The importance of the viewing context when watching sex scenes – and the subsequent possible offence caused – is stressed again in these findings (see Table 25). One-half of all respondents said they strongly agreed that it would be embarrassing to watch homosexual scenes with some of the people they tended to watch television with and a further one in five said they agreed slightly. As other findings about the depiction of sexual activity have suggested, there is also a desire that 'safe' sex should be, in some way, portrayed.

The qualitative findings, indicating the dislike many respondents claimed to feel when watching male homosexual scenes, are further substantiated here. It should be noted that respondents aged over 55 were more likely to 'strongly agree' that they would find the screening of physical contact between men offensive (55 per cent of respondents aged 55 and over said this in comparison with 40 per cent of those aged under 55). Again, this greater strength of feeling of the over 55s was shown in the statement 'Programmes and films about gays and lesbians should be banned' where 36 per cent strongly agreed with the statement in contrast with 25 per cent of the sample as a whole. The antithesis of this statement, and others saying that gay or lesbian characters should not be shown on television, 'Homosexual men and lesbians should be able to see their own programmes' was – as might be expected – agreed with in general by the under 25 year olds and strongly disagreed with by one-third of the respondents aged over 55 who were questioned.

Table 25. General attitudes to the portrayal of homosexuality[7]

	Strongly agree %	Slightly agree %	Slightly disagree %	Strongly disagree %
I would find it embarrassing to watch homosexual sex scenes with some of the people with whom I watch TV	50	21	12	16
It should be made clear that condoms are used in sex scenes showing gay men, to encourage safe sex	48	28	6	18
I would find the screening of any physical contact between gay men offensive	45	17	17	21
Programmes and films about gays and lesbians should be banned	25	14	28	33
Lesbian characters should not be shown on television at all	24	15	28	33
Gay characters should not be shown on television at all	22	16	27	35
Homosexual men and lesbians should be able to see their own programmes	22	36	18	24
It's important to show homosexuality if it's necessary to the story	16	44	16	23
Since homosexuality happens in real life, it's all right to put it on	15	31	21	32
It's all right to show homosexual sex if it's just in one scene, but not if it's all the way through programme	11	29	21	39
I don't mind watching lesbian scenes	10	20	22	48
I don't mind watching gay scenes	9	18	23	50

7   Respondents aged under 17 were not asked this set of questions. The sample size for this, and subsequent tables within this section, is 1049 adults.

It would be wrong to suggest that it was only those aged over 55 who were against the showing of homosexual scenes – other respondents were not so uniform in their concern or embarrassment about the portrayal of homosexual relationships but they did express reservations. Parents of children aged 13 years and over were frequently less positive about the showing of homosexual characters, for example, than either parents of younger children or indeed, the sample as a whole. Over half the respondents questioned agreed that it was acceptable to show homosexuality if it was necessary to the story, but the strength of agreement (16 per cent strongly agreed with this statement) was less definite than that for other statements. Similarly, 15 per cent of respondents agreed strongly that it was all right to show homosexuality as it was a fact of 'real life'. However, half of all respondents were likely to strongly *disagree* with the statements that they did not mind watching gay or lesbian scenes. It is worth noting that young male respondents (under 35 years of age) were more likely to say that they did not mind watching such scenes than female respondents of a similar age.

Despite the findings in the previous table, suggesting a certain degree of reservation, over three-quarters of respondents agreed with the statement 'On television, gay and lesbian characters should be shown to lead their everyday lives, without their sexuality being central to the plot' (Table 26). This greater tolerance reflects the avowed wish of the homosexuals interviewed in the study. Should homosexuality be shown, it should be incidental to the storyline. There was also concern expressed by over half the adult sample interviewed that the representation of homosexual characters should be seen to be 'fair' to that population. This concern about the sensibilities of others echoes earlier findings that respondents did not wish to offend against people's particular beliefs or values.

Table 26. Way in which homosexual characters are represented

	Strongly agree %	Slightly agree %	Slightly disagree %	Strongly disagree %
On television, gay and lesbian characters should be shown to lead their everyday lives, without their sexuality being central to the plot	46	35	7	12
Too much fun is made of gays	27	39	17	17
Gay men and lesbians should be able to see their relationships dealt with fairly on television	24	39	14	22
It's OK to show homosexual sex if it's seen to be in a meaningful relationship	12	28	21	39
Gay men and lesbian women should be on TV to make them more acceptable to society	12	27	25	36

Most respondents agreed that the screening of homosexual scenes should be transmitted after 10.00 pm and two-thirds were concerned that children should not see programmes which contained homosexual characters (Table 27). Again, this finding

echoed the concern expressed in the qualitative research about the possible suscepti-
bility of the child audience. Despite this, one half of the sample was able to agree with
the contradictory statement 'Television has no influence on whether people are
homosexual or heterosexual'.

Table 27. Effect on children

	Strongly agree %	Slightly agree %	Slightly disagree %	Strongly disagree %
Homosexual scenes should only be shown after 10 pm	62	17	6	15
Don't think children should see programmes showing gay and lesbian characters	51	15	14	20
TV has no influence on whether people are homosexual or heterosexual	35	26	19	20

The conflict that many respondents felt between a desire to be seen as tolerant and
broad-minded about sexual matters, and their personal dislike of, or embarrassment
with, depictions of sexual activity is nowhere so clearly seen as in the consideration
of the portrayal of homosexuality. The majority of respondents could accept that
homosexuals should have programming aimed at them, or that programmes could
include homosexual characters, but they were uncertain that such programming
should be transmitted within peak-time viewing hours. They also were generally
definite that children should not have access to any such material. Indeed, parental
permission was not granted to ask questions relating to the statements about homosexuality of the under 17 year olds. Parents did not want their children to be exposed
to such issues.

On the other hand, homosexuals could see the value of television in breaking down
the barriers they felt to be between them and the rest of society. As one respondent
put it:

> 'It's a question of education you know the way it's (homosexuality) portrayed on
> television. There was a programme that had nothing to do with lesbians or gay men
> but there was this character on there who was gay and somebody said "oh, did you
> know he is a poofter?" and all this. The main character was at the bar and said "By
> the way, don't call them poofters, it's offensive". For the main character to say that
> I think is very positive and I think the more that kind of thing's on television the
> better. Television has responsibilities.'
> (Lesbian, Nottingham)

5 Mapping the public

Previous Annual Surveys, and other attitudinal research, have noted that the key differentiators in attitudes and opinions to broadcasting are often the gender of the respondent and his or her age. This Review, concentrating on sex and sexuality, has largely substantiated age as a prime variable and, to a lesser extent, gender. The Council was interested to know if there were any other variables which were key in grouping people with similar attitudes together.

In order to conduct this analysis, a method called 'cluster analysis' was employed. This technique allows the respondent population to be 'mapped' according to their orientation towards a particular subject. In this case, respondents were clustered by shared attitude statements and common characteristics such as, for example, marital status or religious beliefs.

This methodology generated five clusters of respondents who could be classed together and they are described below.

Rejectors: Cluster 1

This cluster, made up of 15 per cent of the sample, was comprised mainly of older (over 55 years old) women who were or had been married and who felt that there was too much sex shown on television. It was also the group most likely to say that sex on television, in particular, was of concern. This group had a slight bias towards respondents from the North of England and Northern Ireland.

The rejectors felt that the depiction of sex on television was offensive, and also that it sanctioned immoral behaviour. Indeed they were likely to agree with most of the statements suggesting that television had a negative effect on the young, and felt that rape scenes should never be shown.

This cluster differed from all the other clusters in its criticism of the statements that suggested it was acceptable to show sex because it was a reality of life; that more explicit sex could be shown on video; that the portrayal of sex was of positive benefit to the young by raising opportunities for discussion and enabling the educative process. This group also disagreed with the comment that people who did not like to see sex on television could turn off. They did not agree that there was any clear

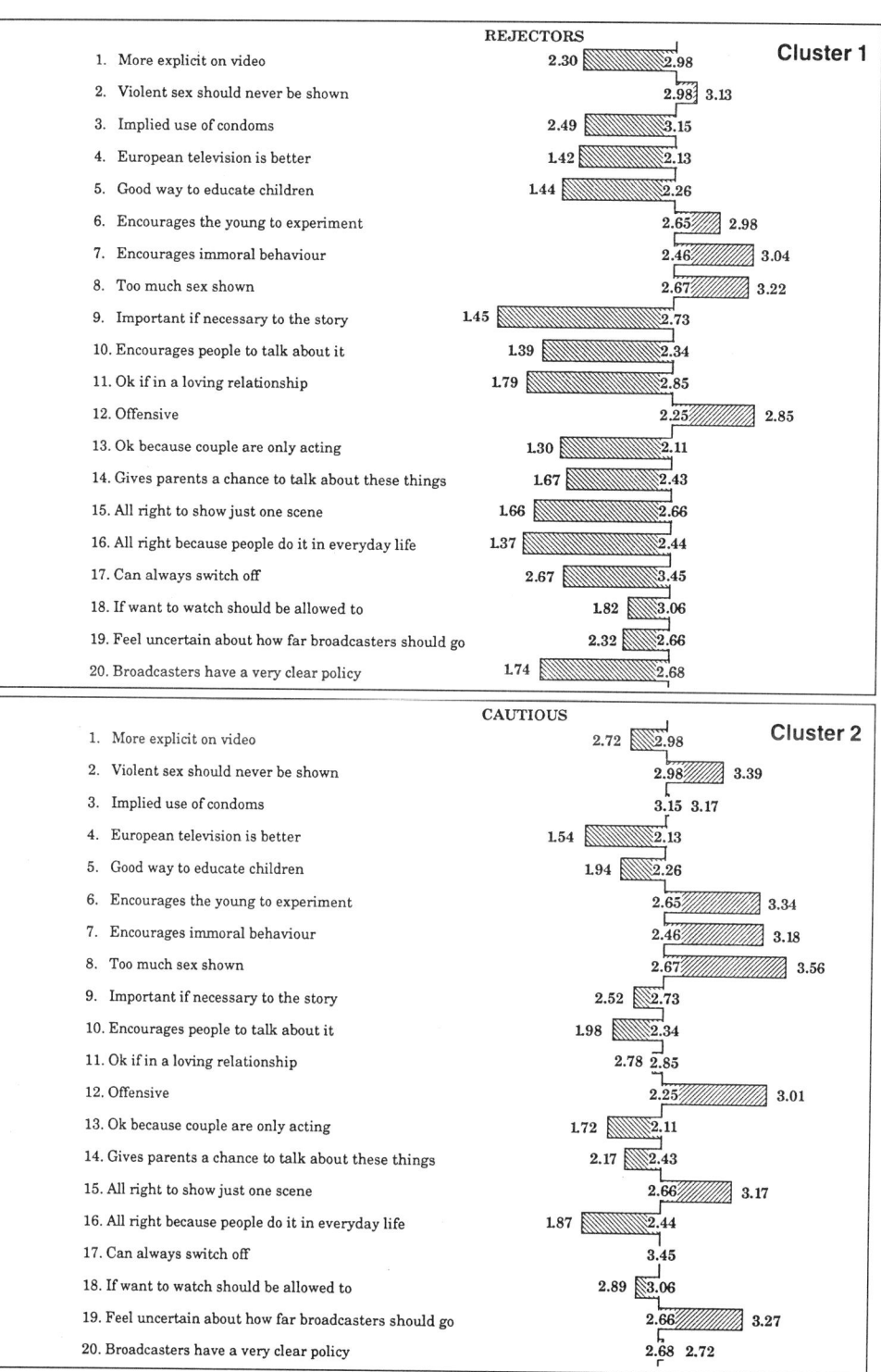

REJECTORS **Cluster 1**

1. More explicit on video — 2.30 | 2.98
2. Violent sex should never be shown — 2.98 | 3.13
3. Implied use of condoms — 2.49 | 3.15
4. European television is better — 1.42 | 2.13
5. Good way to educate children — 1.44 | 2.26
6. Encourages the young to experiment — 2.65 | 2.98
7. Encourages immoral behaviour — 2.46 | 3.04
8. Too much sex shown — 2.67 | 3.22
9. Important if necessary to the story — 1.45 | 2.73
10. Encourages people to talk about it — 1.39 | 2.34
11. Ok if in a loving relationship — 1.79 | 2.85
12. Offensive — 2.25 | 2.85
13. Ok because couple are only acting — 1.30 | 2.11
14. Gives parents a chance to talk about these things — 1.67 | 2.43
15. All right to show just one scene — 1.66 | 2.66
16. All right because people do it in everyday life — 1.37 | 2.44
17. Can always switch off — 2.67 | 3.45
18. If want to watch should be allowed to — 1.82 | 3.06
19. Feel uncertain about how far broadcasters should go — 2.32 | 2.66
20. Broadcasters have a very clear policy — 1.74 | 2.68

CAUTIOUS **Cluster 2**

1. More explicit on video — 2.72 | 2.98
2. Violent sex should never be shown — 2.98 | 3.39
3. Implied use of condoms — 3.15 | 3.17
4. European television is better — 1.54 | 2.13
5. Good way to educate children — 1.94 | 2.26
6. Encourages the young to experiment — 2.65 | 3.34
7. Encourages immoral behaviour — 2.46 | 3.18
8. Too much sex shown — 2.67 | 3.56
9. Important if necessary to the story — 2.52 | 2.73
10. Encourages people to talk about it — 1.98 | 2.34
11. Ok if in a loving relationship — 2.78 | 2.85
12. Offensive — 2.25 | 3.01
13. Ok because couple are only acting — 1.72 | 2.11
14. Gives parents a chance to talk about these things — 2.17 | 2.43
15. All right to show just one scene — 2.66 | 3.17
16. All right because people do it in everyday life — 1.87 | 2.44
17. Can always switch off — 3.45
18. If want to watch should be allowed to — 2.89 | 3.06
19. Feel uncertain about how far broadcasters should go — 2.66 | 3.27
20. Broadcasters have a very clear policy — 2.68 | 2.72

61

broadcasting policy about the portrayal of sexual activity and felt the depiction of sex in almost any context (even, for example, in a loving relationship) was unacceptable. Nor did this group agree that the use of condoms should be implied or that the European attitude towards sex was a preferable one.

It is worth noting that this cluster was significantly more likely than the sample as a whole to have turned the television off either because they were watching something with a child which they felt to be unsuitable (64 per cent of this group said this in comparison with 39 per cent of the general sample), or because they felt personally disgusted (52 per cent said this was a reason for turning off the television or changing channels, in comparison with 27 per cent of the total sample).

Cautious: Cluster 2

Like the rejectors, this group was made up predominantly of female respondents over 55 years of age. They were either married or had been married (and were now widowed, separated or divorced) and had adult children. They were more likely to attend religious services on a regular basis and felt that there was too much sex on television these days. Indeed, sex on television was of most concern to this cluster, which formed 21 per cent of the sample.

While not as condemnatory as the rejectors of cluster 1, these respondents were generally in agreement with the statements that said rape should never be shown on television; that sex on television encouraged children to behave immorally; that they found the portrayal of sex on television offensive and that they were not sure how far the broadcasters should go. They were also likely to think that, if sex was shown at all, it should be only in one scene in a programme. They disagreed with the statement that it was acceptable to show sex on television because it was a reality of life and with the comment that the European 'open' attitude to sex was better than the British attitude.

Moderates: Cluster 3

This cluster accounted for 25 per cent of the sample and, as such, was the largest individual cluster.

Gender was not a significant factor for this group, but it tended to be comprised of those aged under 55 years of age and there were more unmarried respondents in this cluster than for the others. On the whole this group thought that there was about the right amount of sex on television these days and were likely to be in agreement with the statements which suggested that video could show more explicit sex than television; that, if sex was an important part of the story, it should be shown; that sexual activity portrayed in a loving relationship, in particular, was acceptable. These respondents were also particularly likely to agree that showing one scene with sexual activity in a programme was very acceptable and that people who did not want to watch the depiction of sex could turn the television off. The moderates were less certain how far broadcasters should go in the portrayal of sex although they thought there was a clear policy being followed. Finally, this group was likely to agree that condoms should be shown to be used in sex scenes.

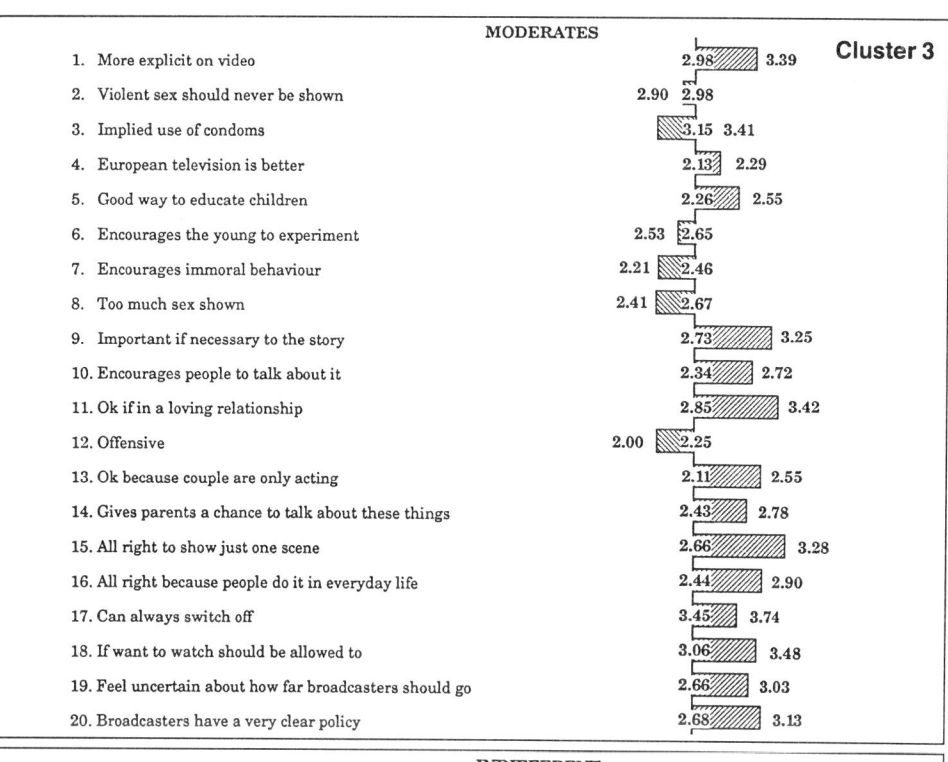

MODERATES — Cluster 3

1.	More explicit on video	2.98	3.39
2.	Violent sex should never be shown	2.90	2.98
3.	Implied use of condoms	3.15	3.41
4.	European television is better	2.13	2.29
5.	Good way to educate children	2.26	2.55
6.	Encourages the young to experiment	2.53	2.65
7.	Encourages immoral behaviour	2.21	2.46
8.	Too much sex shown	2.41	2.67
9.	Important if necessary to the story	2.73	3.25
10.	Encourages people to talk about it	2.34	2.72
11.	Ok if in a loving relationship	2.85	3.42
12.	Offensive	2.00	2.25
13.	Ok because couple are only acting	2.11	2.55
14.	Gives parents a chance to talk about these things	2.43	2.78
15.	All right to show just one scene	2.66	3.28
16.	All right because people do it in everyday life	2.44	2.90
17.	Can always switch off	3.45	3.74
18.	If want to watch should be allowed to	3.06	3.48
19.	Feel uncertain about how far broadcasters should go	2.66	3.03
20.	Broadcasters have a very clear policy	2.68	3.13

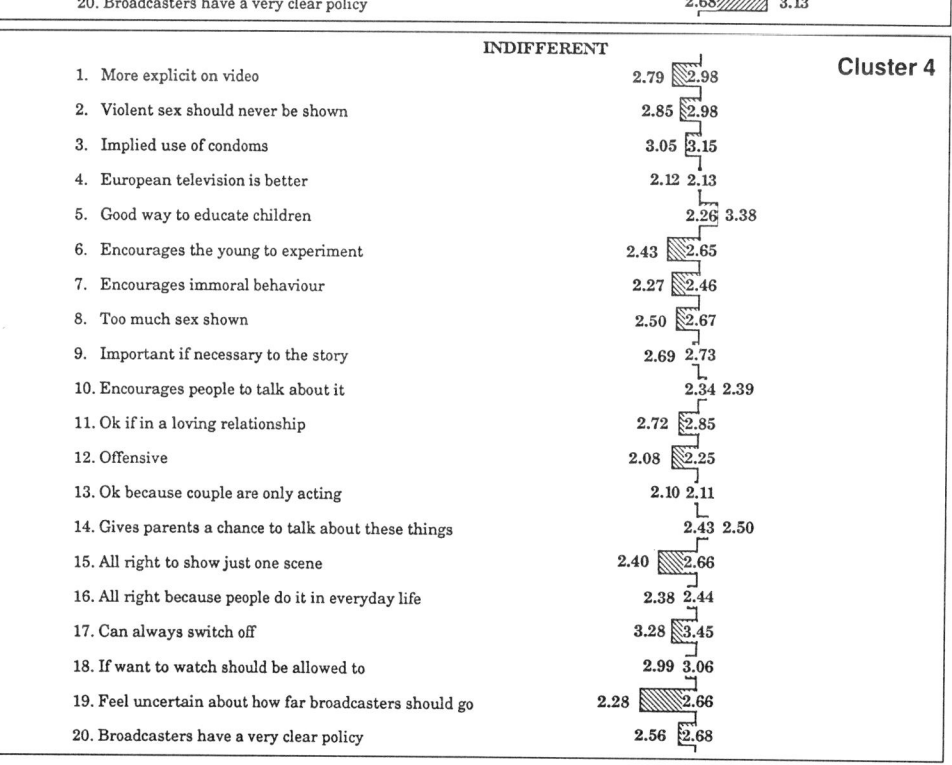

INDIFFERENT — Cluster 4

1.	More explicit on video	2.79	2.98
2.	Violent sex should never be shown	2.85	2.98
3.	Implied use of condoms	3.05	3.15
4.	European television is better	2.12	2.13
5.	Good way to educate children	2.26	3.38
6.	Encourages the young to experiment	2.43	2.65
7.	Encourages immoral behaviour	2.27	2.46
8.	Too much sex shown	2.50	2.67
9.	Important if necessary to the story	2.69	2.73
10.	Encourages people to talk about it	2.34	2.39
11.	Ok if in a loving relationship	2.72	2.85
12.	Offensive	2.08	2.25
13.	Ok because couple are only acting	2.10	2.11
14.	Gives parents a chance to talk about these things	2.43	2.50
15.	All right to show just one scene	2.40	2.66
16.	All right because people do it in everyday life	2.38	2.44
17.	Can always switch off	3.28	3.45
18.	If want to watch should be allowed to	2.99	3.06
19.	Feel uncertain about how far broadcasters should go	2.28	2.66
20.	Broadcasters have a very clear policy	2.56	2.68

Indifferent: Cluster 4

This group formed the second largest cluster of respondents, being 23 per cent of the sample.

As with the moderates, gender was not a significant differentiating factor in this group, but they were more likely to be aged between 35–54 years of age. This cluster had a relatively high proportion of people from the social class C1 within it, and a South of England bias. Like the moderates, these respondents felt that there was about the right amount of sex on television these days. The important variable about this group was that they had no strong feelings about any of the statements which suggested that certain parameters could increase the acceptability of a scene depicting sexual activity, but were largely indifferent to all of them.

Permissives: Cluster 5

The final cluster, the permissives, was made up of 16 per cent of the sample. Seventy per cent of this group was male and over eighty per cent were aged between 18 and 54 years of age. It had a South of England bias and nearly one in three respondents were of the social class, C2. Many respondents in this group had children aged under seven years of age. They were less likely than the other clusters to practice a religion and were also quite likely to say that there was 'too little' or 'about the right amount' of sex on television. One quarter of the respondents in this cluster owned satellite receivers.

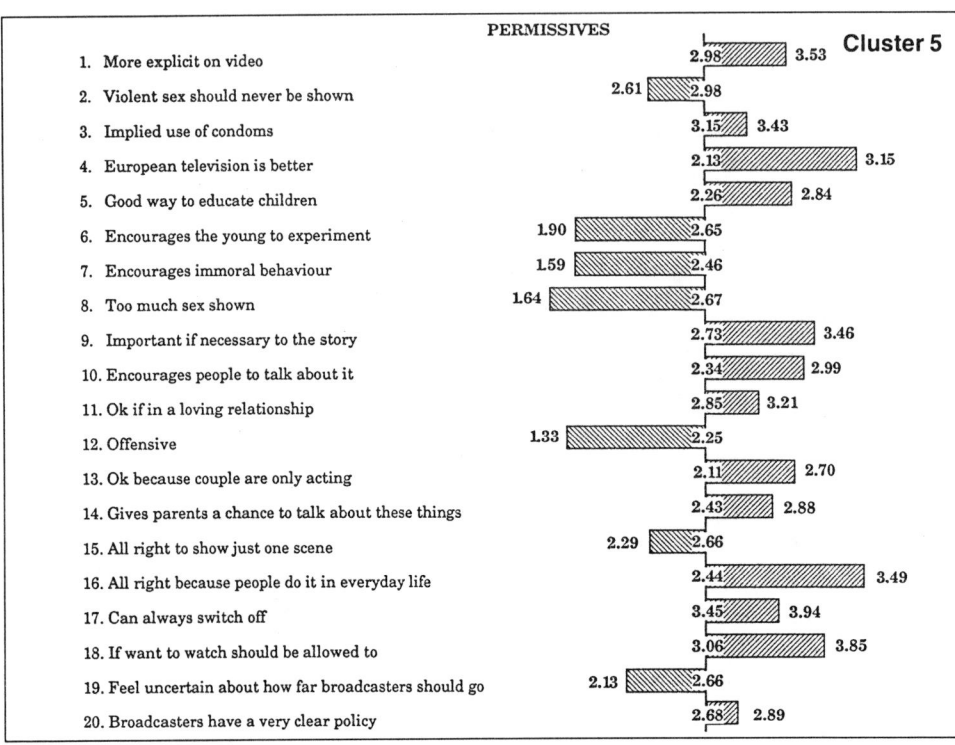

The permissives were more likely to agree with the comments which said that those who were offended by sex on television, could turn the television off; that more explicit sex can be shown on video and that the more 'open' European attitude was better. They were also likely to agree that the portrayal of sex on television could be a good way to educate children (and agreed that the use of condoms should be implied in sex scenes) and that it encouraged parents and children to talk together. There was agreement that it was important to show sex if it was important to the story; that it should be shown in a loving relationship and was a natural part of life. This group also concurred that it was permissible to show the depiction of sex because it was not real, but acting.

On the other hand, this group did not feel that the portrayal of sex on television encouraged immoral behaviour or early experimentation; they did not find sex scenes on television offensive and did not agree that rape scenes should never be shown on television.

When asked to name a factor in television broadcasting which caused them most concern, this group was twice as likely as any of the other clusters to say 'none'. They were also the group most likely to say that they had never switched off the television set, or changed channels, because they were disgusted by something they had seen.

6 Content analysis

Introduction

The Council was interested to know how British television depicted sex in the 1990s and asked the Communications Research Group, based at Aston University, to undertake one week's content analysis of television programming so that the actual output of television during the main viewing hours could be monitored for the depiction of sexual activity and sexuality.

Few studies exist outside North America where the most common finding has been that, while sexual intercourse was often mentioned, frequently by characters not married to one another, visual depiction was scarce and was – without exception – discreet. 'Deviant' sexual activity was found to be extremely rare and could always be isolated to a specific programme. These studies in the US also found that there was little difference in the level of physical intimacy shown before and after Family Viewing Time (the American equivalent of the Watershed).

It was to investigate parameters such as these that this content analysis was undertaken. The sample covered all output on the four terrestrial television channels (BBC1, BBC2, ITV and Channel Four) between 18.00 hours to 24.00 hours for each of seven days starting on Monday 13 January 1992.

In total 277 programmes and 524 advertisements were analysed and the data presented below are based on these.

Sexual activity

Fifty seven scenes of sexual activity were noted. All portrayed heterosexual sex. As Table 27 below shows, the amount of detail shown varied quite considerably.

Over half of the scenes portrayed kissing with obvious sexual intent, while just under one-quarter depicted the coital act. Other scenes were noted to be pre-coital (if the camera had stayed with the scene the depiction of sexual intercourse might have been expected to occur) or post-coital. There were also two scenes noted (from two different programmes) where sex was implied through sound although the characters could not be seen, and the one scene of 'metaphorical' sex referred to in the table was in a film where the 'crashing waves' in Alan Plater's essay were enhanced by a train entering a tunnel and fireworks, all accompanied by music.

Table 28. Type of sexual activity by channel

	BBC1		BBC2		ITV		C4		Total	
	N	%	N	%	N	%	N	%	N	%
Kissing	4	27	9	60	9	69	8	57	30	53
Metaphorical	–	–	1	7	–	–	–	–	1	2
Implied	–	–	1	7	–	–	1	7	2	4
Pre-coital	2	13	2	13	1	7	1	7	6	11
Post-coital	2	13	–	–	–	–	3	21	5	9
Coital act	7	47	2	13	3	23	1	7	12	23
TOTAL	15	100	15	100	13	99	14	99	57	102

Over one-third (35 per cent) of the relationships in which some sexual activity occurred were established relationships, although few were marital. Nearly one-quarter of the other relationships were extra-marital affairs where the male partner was committing adultery (see Table 29 below).

Table 29. Context of sexual activity

Type of relationship	Number	%
Established married	5	9
Established non-married	15	26
Extra-marital affair: man	13	23
Extra-marital affair: woman	1	2
Extra-marital affair: both	1	2
1st time pick up by male	3	5
1st time pick up by female	3	5
1st time pick up mutual	6	11
Rape or sexual abuse	1	2
Prostitution	2	4
Other	7	12
Total	57	101

The rape scene mentioned here was the scene from *A Time To Dance.*

It is worth noting that, when respondents to the quantitative research were considering the scenarios, they had made some negative comment about the adulterous nature of some of them. However, respondents talking more generally in the group discussions did not mention the nature or type of relationship as being an important variable when they were talking about the way in which they felt sex should be depicted. As a counterpoint, the content analysis suggested that, in fact, many of the sexual relationships represented on television are portrayed within 'established', if not marital, relationships. Nevertheless, a significant number of the liaisons were extra-marital. In this context it is interesting to note the 1990 British Social Attitudes Survey examined the opinions of people to both pre-marital and extra-marital affairs, and found that the former were now largely accepted while the latter were still felt to be wrong by a significant majority of respondents (see Table 30).

Table 30. Attitudes to pre-marital and extra-marital relationships

If a man and woman have sexual relations before marriage, what would your general opinion be?

	%
Always wrong	13
Mostly wrong	10
Sometimes wrong	24
Rarely wrong	9
Not wrong at all	45

What about a married person having sexual relations with someone other than his or her partner?

	%
Always wrong	56
Mostly wrong	29
Sometimes wrong	12
Rarely wrong	1
Not wrong at all	2

Source: SCPR 1990

The content analysis found that warnings prior to transmission were rarely direct and explicit. Rather they referred to 'powerful and passionate emotions' or ' the powerful tale of a compulsive and tempestuous love affair' or, even, 'adult comedy'. Despite such warnings, two-thirds of the scenes were expected because of the dramatic build-up to them. The remainder were either coded as unexpected (such as the rape scene in *A Time To Dance*) or irrelevant to the plot (for example, in the film *Thunderbolt and Lightfoot*, where two incidental characters were having sex and a principal character burst into their room).

One in five of all the sex scenes occurred before the Watershed at 9.00 pm but they were mild (showing kissing with sexual intent or metaphorical sex) and all were noted to be relevant to the story-line.

Few (less than one in ten) of the programmes which included depictions of sexual activity or nudity (see below) referred to contraception or sexually transmitted diseases. Four of the seven programmes within the sample which did refer to AIDS or to the HIV virus were factual programmes and the other three were dramas – none of these portrayed either nudity or sexual activity.

The scenes were fairly evenly split between UK – and USA – produced programmes.

Character profiles were completed for all those characters participating in sexual activity who also spoke. In all but one programme (a US-produced police series), the characters were white and in all but one programme (a UK-produced play), the characters were able-bodied. Most (70 per cent) of the characters profiled played major roles and over half of them (55 per cent) were in serious parts. Only one in ten were in essentially comic roles.

Nudity

During the period that the broadcasts were monitored, 65 scenes were noted with nude people. Overall nude females outnumbered nude males by a ratio of 3:2.

For each scene depicting nudity, note was made of the part of the body that was exposed and the level of exposure. One-third of the instances of nudity were of female breasts; one-fifth of instances were male buttocks ; and nearly the same proportion of female buttocks were noted and while nearly one in ten of the instances showed a female full frontal, no instance of a male full frontal was recorded.

Table 31 shows the context in which the nude scene occurred.

Table 31. Context of nudity

	Number	%
Natural, indoor	10	15
Natural, outdoor	5	8
Photograph, painting, statue	3	5
Normal (for culture)	30	46
Other	4	6
	13	20
Total	65	100

One-half of all scenes which showed nudity were scenes showing paintings, photographs or sculpture. (Some of the programmes showing such visual material were serious arts programmes while one was a film in which a character was surprised while reading a pornographic magazine and some of the pictures from the magazine were shown). In the scenes coded as 'other', the programmes included nudity for reasons of example (as in current affairs programmes) or nudity in film clips, taken out of context, but used as back-up for the presenter.

Most of the nudity could be anticipated due to the subject under consideration, or the developing story-line. The scenes were split evenly between those shown before and after the Watershed – those noted before 9.00 pm were scenes in serious arts programming or in the news.

The majority of the scenes (83 per cent) were in UK-produced programming.

References and allusions to sex and nudity

These were divided into two main categories – those which were direct references to sex or nudity and those which were double entendres or puns. As one might expect, most of the latter category were to be found in comedy programmes (89 per cent of all such allusions) and the majority (82 per cent) were in programmes broadcast before the Watershed.

Direct references to sex and nudity were less frequent (being noted in 45 cases) and over half of them were in comedy or light entertainment programmes. Where references were made in serious programming, they often formed a light interlude in the narration or action. Most of the direct references (69 per cent) occurred after the Watershed, in contrast to the oblique references noted earlier.

Incidence of non-heterosexual characters

The content analysis recorded those characters who were homosexual, bisexual or were implied to be either homosexual or bisexual. They were recognized by overt statements or behaviour, and the implied sexuality of characters – if non-heterosexual – was identified by behaviour or oblique references to their sexual orientation.

In this sample, seventeen characters were classified in this way, and were drawn from eight programmes. Of these seventeen characters, six were recorded as 'implied homosexual' rather than overtly homosexual as they depicted the stereotypical ('camp') behaviour which is often associated with perceived homosexual behaviour. Of these implied homosexual characters, four were in comic roles (covering three programmes). The remaining two were in dramas, portraying characters involved in the Arts.

Two of the seventeen people were identified as bisexual – one classified himself as such in a factual interview programme, and one was a fictional character in a film.

The remainder of the characters (nine in total) were coded as homosexual and were all drawn from two programmes; one a drama dealing with a homosexual relationship and the other a film which dealt with the blackmailing of homosexuals in the days when homosexuality was illegal in the UK.

Summary

The content analyses that were available from the US for comparison with the content analysis undertaken for this Review would suggest that British television was more explicit in the level of detail that was shown on prime-time television. Nonetheless all depiction remained quite discreet, although nudity was more prevalent than on American television.

As the American analyses had found, sexual relationships were often presented as between people who were not married to one another. There was some reference made, in the programmes monitored for the Review, to contraception and sexually transmitted diseases, although this was rare.

Finally, while the data are not directly comparable, it is worth noting that there would appear to be greater notice paid to the Watershed and the consideration of children as part of the audience in British television than in the scheduling of programmes in the US (certainly in the 1980s).

7 Conclusions

This research, and other studies that have gone before it, have pointed to the particular nature of the relationship the viewer or listener has with broadcasting. There is the notion of a 'contract' between the broadcaster and his audience which ensures that, as long as certain customs are followed, most of the audience will allow the broadcaster considerable licence in what is transmitted. These customs are founded on understood concepts of scheduling (based, for television, on the principle of the Watershed); a knowledge of programme genres and the material they will contain; and the adequate labelling of programmes that might vary from that which is expected.

This Review has also found, however, that a specific tension exists between the respondent's desire to be open and tolerant of matters sexual in general – which translates into a wish to be tolerant of the depiction of sexual activity on television -and the feeling of embarrassment or offence or concern for minors and other vulnerable groups that can occur when watching or listening to portrayals of sexual activity, even in private and on one's own.

This contrasts with the attitudes of respondents to issues related to the portrayal of violence or matters of taste and decency in broadcasting. Respondents would appear to find these less complicated issues to deal with, often expressing greater concern about them than about depictions of sexual activity. Nonetheless, it is the sexual content of programmes that is more likely to make the viewer or listener reach for the 'off' button or change channels.

Embarrassment is more likely to be caused if parents are watching with children, particularly as the children approach, or reach, puberty. However, the embarrassment would appear to be two-way with children admitting (although less frequently) to discomfort when watching sex scenes on television while their parents were also there. Much of the uneasiness came from uncertainty about the level of the child's sexual knowledge, and so it was lessened as the children became parents themselves.

In many cases, respondents admitted to using distractions to draw attention away from the screen while there was something embarrassing on but the learned rules of timing and scheduling usually allowed avoidance, if required.

In addition to these understood conventions of scheduling which sought to ensure that children, in particular, were protected from seeing material considered unsuitable, should be added expectations based on a knowledge of programme genres. This Review has illustrated how much the different genres can affect the respondent's perception of the acceptability of a particular sex scene; there are clear distinctions made about the appropriateness of a scene depicting sexual activity in a drama, for example, in comparison with a situation comedy.

There were certain other variables which affected the acceptability of a particular scene depicting sexual activity. For example, respondents felt strongly that the sex should be seen to have a role to play in the unfolding of the plot, to be relevant to the storyline. There were also certain niceties to be observed within the nature of the relationships portrayed; respondents voiced concerns about the role models that television might offer, particularly to the young. In addition, the type of sexual activity portrayed should fall within certain boundaries. This latter point was especially important when the depiction of homosexuality was being discussed. Other variables, such as knowledge of the author or playwright, were also judged to be important in increasing acceptance of a sexual scene within a programme.

Respondents did feel that there was more sex depicted on television these days and that the boundaries were being pushed back. The tension already described made them uncertain about their reaction to this. But, in each case,there was no clear set of rules that could be laid down – indeed, most respondents would not have wanted that to happen. Instead, different variables could coexist to make a particular scene more acceptable than one might otherwise have thought. The boundary that should not be transgressed, it was generally agreed, was that set by the Watershed. There was also concern that the Watershed at 9.00 pm should not be seen by the broadcaster as an absolute – a time at which all young children should be considered to be in bed – but that programming should gradually become more 'adult' as the evening progressed.

Radio broadcasts elicited fewer concerns than television; it seemed less likely to cause offence and the solitary nature of much radio listening is likely to be a factor in this finding.

It may also be of interest to note again the different reactions that the individual scenarios drew. Scenario 3, a dramatized documentary in which a younger boy was seduced, drew great criticism. This was despite the fact that the scene occurred within a drama-documentary which was scheduled late in the evening, well after the Watershed. The transmission time should have removed many objections and documentaries were usually allowed considerable freedom. Respondents seemed to react against the idea that a young person had been seduced but, more than that, they seemed to be reacting against the *reconstruction* of the seduction scene, despite the fact that it was not explicit. They were possibly questioning the need to show any part of the physical act. There is also a strong possibility, based on the findings of the Review, that they were reacting against the homosexual aspect of the seduction.

In contrast, the programme described by Scenario 6 was thought, by most respondents, to be very acceptable. It was transmitted early in the evening and considered a difficult subject – the abuse of a child – but the fact that it was a documentary and was seen not to 'dramatize' the subject, coupled with the knowledge that it was on radio, made it easier to allow.

Not all homosexuality was frowned upon although many respondents did admit to discomfort with its portrayal. However, there was agreement among some respondents (regardless of their sexuality) that a character's homosexuality should not be an issue, unless it was pivotal to the plot, but should be allowed to emerge as the character developed. This was particularly felt to be the case with a genre such as the soap opera.

Finally, an objective look at television's output (in the form of a content analysis) showed that many of these wishes were respected – programmes depicting sexual activity occurred after the Watershed, in relevant genres and the relationships portrayed were generally established. However, a content analysis could not capture the other contextual considerations that might make a scene depicting sex acceptable and the Review has sought to illustrate what these might be.

ESSAYS

Sex, television drama and the writer

by Alan Plater

L et us begin, in every sense, at the beginning. The sexual act, in an ideal world, is the supreme form of personal communion, an intimate celebration of love, joy, tenderness and the human spirit.

But we do not live in an ideal world, and too often sex is perverted, most commonly as something done to women by men. In D. H. Lawrence's phrase, men do the dirty on sex. All sexual activity dwells somewhere between these extremes: between Love and Rape: between gentle sharing and savage exploitation; and since it is the duty of writers to bear witness to the key conflicts of human experience, sex has a vital place in the drama we place on the record.

So far, so worthy. But honesty compels me to report, as a writer of dramatic fiction for radio, television, films and theatre for thirty years, that sex has never given me serious problems. The reason is simple; for me the great tragi-comic drama of sex lies not in the act itself, but in the psychological paraphernalia with which we surround it. The question is not: will A go to bed with B or C? The question is: what will be the effect of that decision on the person excluded? The drama lies in the anticipation – the foreplay, if you will – and in the consequences. The act itself, as Noel Coward pointed out, is frequently ludicrous to all except the participants.

In this respect, sex has a function parallel to the McGuffin in a Hitchcock thriller. He explained it thus:

> '... the "McGuffin" is the term we use to cover ... the secret plans or documents ... the logicians are wrong in trying to figure out the truth of a McGuffin, since it's beside the point. The only thing that matters is that ... the plans, documents or secrets must seem to be of vital importance to the characters.'

Sex as McGuffin recurs throughout the history of drama and its importance, almost invariably, is in its effect on other people: tragically in *Othello*, where the sex takes place in the mind of the protagonists: farcically and off-stage in Feydeau or Ben Travers; but traumatically and necessarily on-screen in Dennis Potter's *The Singing*

Detective, where the boy's glimpse of his mother's extra-marital sexual encounter is a crucial element in a complex, multi-level narrative.

And goodness, what a fuss that scene created! In 1987, I was part of a Writers' Guild delegation which met Gerald Howarth, MP, who was preparing a Private Member's Bill (later buried in the turmoil of the General Election) aimed at extending the Obscenity Laws to cover Broadcasting. *The Singing Detective* was high on the agenda.

'Have you seen it?' we asked. It seemed a reasonable question in the circumstances. It emerged that he hadn't, but Mrs Whitehouse had played a tape of edited highlights for the benefit of selected Parliamentarians.

As we understood it, the Whitehouse proposition was – and maybe still is – that a glimpse of buttocks and/or breasts was likely to implant unworthy thoughts in susceptible minds: that previously innocent voters who hitherto had never given serious thought to buttocks and breasts would suddenly think: 'Wow! That's for me!' and rush out in search of the real thing. Perhaps the Honourable Members who saw the video did that but if so, it was not reported in the national press.

This may seem a facetious analysis; but there is no evidence, scientific or anecdotal, that sexually repressed citizens, needing to sustain their masturbatory fantasies, scan the pages of *Radio Times* in search of the latest work by Dennis Potter. The sad truth – and truth doesn't come much sadder – is that such people go to their corner shop to buy a pornographic magazine or rent a dirty video; and sooner rather than later they will have satellite channels beaming in blue movies twenty-four hours a day. That is the logical conclusion of deregulated, market-driven television: at the end of the line is a warehouse full of cheap movies doing the dirty on sex, and doing it violently.

Historically, writers have always claimed that controversial moments must be judged by the contribution to the whole. It was true of *Pygmalion* and of *Lady Chatterley's Lover*, and it remains our primary defence of scenes with a sexual content. Predictably, our critics are generally more concerned with what makes the best headline than with the protection of the body politic.

Alan Bleasdale's magnificent series, *GBH*, caused a predictable uproar, but the hacks settled on 'Is Michael Murray really Derek Hatton?' as their designated lead story, thus overlooking what was an extraordinary and possibly unique depiction of on-screen sex: a view from within, no less. A bedroom scene involving Lindsay Duncan as Barbara Douglas and Robert Lindsay as Murray included a moment when Douglas made a tender speech addressed to Murray's penis, a part played on this occasion by the camera – in technical terms, a subjective camera shot. It was a remarkable moment, which took us into the heart of the situation, gave a poignant insight into the characters at that stage in the drama and, above all, was hilariously *funny*.

This is one of our trade secrets: you can get away with anything, including murder, if you make it funny. Hitchcock made a career out of it. In 1975 I wrote a series called *Trinity Tales* for BBC Television, inspired by Chaucer's great original. Our modern pilgrims travelled to Wembley for the Rugby League Cup Final. On the way they had adventures and told each other stories.

As in Chaucer, some of the stories were rude with a high incidence of bed-hopping, but using the McGuffin principle, our key dramatic element was never the sexual act, but its impact on the narrative. Our technique was to wait until the moment of initial physical embrace then cut away to visuals of waves lashing on a sea-shore, in the best cheapskate Hollywood tradition. These days the smarter critics would call it 'de-constructing the genre' but we were just having fun. Then, during the final climactic coupling in our version of *The Miller's Tale*, one of the participants says: 'Hey up! Here come the waves again!'

Curiously enough, I had used a similar technique in 1970, unsmilingly, in a film version of D. H. Lawrence's *The Virgin and Gypsy*, a serious and beautiful study of young girl's sexual awakening. Essentially it is a Sleeping Beauty plot – a recurring motif in Lawrence. The girl's awakening, in the arms of the eponymous hero, coincides with a mighty flood that destroys the vicarage where she lives. Lawrence is never mean with his symbolism.

The movie is modest and gentle, with occasional, nicely-composed arrangements of buttocks and breasts, sometimes in slow motion, but tactful and restrained. If Ken Russell's version of *Women in Love* was Wagnerian, we were closer to Delius.

Nonetheless, I was waiting for a train on the Central Line one day soon after the film had opened and found myself standing beside a large poster including selected press quotes. One of them said: 'the finest sex film ever made' – so I moved along the platform in search of a more innocuous poster to stand beside.

That might seem like the confession of an unprincipled adolescent, still sniggering behind the cycle sheds in middle age. *Mea culpa*, some of the time anyway. We all retain this element within us, including people who sit on very important committees; I have sat on very important committees and know. But we must try very hard to be grown-up.

The problem, for writers and law-makers alike, is that life never keeps still. When I started writing for radio in 1961, we were forbidden to mention any trade names in the dialogue, with the exception of Rolls Royce. Today England's international footballers and cricketers appear on network television looking more like advertising supplements than professional sportsmen. In sexual terms, even ten years ago it would have been impossible to use the word 'condom' in the dialogue of a television play. Today it is more or less compulsory, whereas the tired and trusted 1960s stage direction: 'he lights a cigarette' has disappeared without trace. So it goes, as Mr Vonnegut says, and it is going faster all the time.

It is our job as dramatists to make the global kaleidoscope keep still long enough to ask a few impertinent questions, though we do not kid ourselves we have any answers. The convention is to say that drama must reflect real life; but that seems to me a limited and limiting view. Our job is not reflection but *refraction*: dividing up the white light into its constituent colours. Peter Nichols describes the process as making dreams useful.

The colours in the spectrum vary from writer to writer: that is why we have writers. A painter shows us what the world looks like, a composer what it sounds like, a dramatist what it feels like. It is to the credit of British television that writers – unlike our American colleagues – are still allowed to leave individual fingerprints on their work. For years we were encouraged to do so and from my admittedly prejudiced point of view, the success of our programmes, artistic and commercial, though strictly in that order, has largely been writer-based.

Original drama from the John Hopkins quarter, *Talking to A Stranger* to *GBH*: popular series from *Z Cars* to *Inspector Morse*: dramatizations from *I Claudius* to *Anglo-Saxon Attitudes*: situation comedies from *Hancock* to *Fawlty Towers*; in the beginning of all of them were some very good words indeed.

Each of a hundred or more writers like Hopkins, Bleasdale, Andrew Davies or Alan Bennett, offers a unique vision of the world: a personal, sometimes idiosyncratic bundle of concerns and passions. Mine, for the record, include jazz, football, Geordies, vintage music-hall jokes and the long shadow of the Industrial Revolution. Under-lying these are the universal themes that govern all our work: Love, Birth, Growth, Death, War, Work and, inevitably and properly, Sex.

It has its place in every writer's spectrum, crucially so in programmes like *The Singing Detective*, marginally in *GBH*, classically in *I Claudius*, rustically in *Trinity Tales*, conspicuously but significantly absent in *Inspector Morse*.

On the rare occasions that sex becomes a problem, it relates to the way writing happens at the desk. Good writing, as J. B. Priestley pointed out, comes from the back of the head, not from the front. We draw on a deep well of memory and observation. We trust the sub-conscious and, ultimately, trust our characters to tell their story. If they do not, you are in trouble. But if they do, you may also be in trouble because occasionally they say or do something likely to offend susceptible elements with friends in high places.

At that point, the writer switches off the sub-conscious and calls upon the front of the head for some cool, professional thinking. Assuming the sub-conscious has thrown up a sexually explosive moment, the analysis might run:

> Is this explosive moment crucial to the drama? If it is removed, does the entire narrative/thematic/psychological edifice collapse? Is a McGuffin approach possible? Can I move the moment off-stage? Can we cut away to waves lashing on the sea-shore or use some other cheap gag? Is there another way of creating the same effect? If there is no other way and I deliver the scene as written, am I prepared to fight the necessary battles with the producer? And if the producer agrees with me, will the producer be prepared to fight the necessary battles with network controllers, co-producers, boards of directors and/or governors, pressure groups, plus the other regulatory bodies that control our destinies? Even, all the Gods forbid, commercial sponsors? It is a matter of historical record that sponsors murdered original American television drama forty years ago. You cannot ask impertinent questions and sell cheese at the same time.

It may surprise some people, but writers do not rush to the barricades in the manner described. It is not fun and the writer invariably loses. I have been censored once only, a bitter experience that consumed more time and energy than any of the participants could spare. It was not, incidentally, over a sexual issue.

Over the years, every writer accumulates a ragbag of experience, a mixture of small triumphs and hard-luck stories, tiny betrayals and old regrets: it is the best we can offer in the way of a professional creed. Mine includes the following:

The sexual act, to repeat, is potentially the supreme form of personal communion, an intimate celebration of love, joy, tenderness and the human spirit. It is frequently perverted, at which point it no longer celebrates life but anticipates death. At both extremes it places people on the outer edge of experience where they most clearly define themselves. Drama flourishes best on these precipices.

But drama is a performance art and I do not have the right to humiliate actors for the benefit of the camera. The script should indicate, clearly and unambiguously, what the actor is expected to do; and the actor has an inalienable right to refuse.

How many times has this happened to me in thirty years? Never.

All drama is based on illusion. The wooden *O* becomes the battlefield of Agincourt and it is easy, if the words are right. The camera and the film editor between them are skilful and compulsive liars, and there is a huge gap between what the audience *thinks* it has seen and what happened on the day of shooting. The American film industry slaughters characters in their thousands annually without killing too many actors.

That, then, is the creed. Tell the truth, while protecting the dignity of the performer. It is remarkably straightforward, as creeds go. Nobody is likely to go to war over it, which is more than can be said for most creeds. The fact is, sex and sexuality are not a major problem for writers working within a decent public service tradition; they are more likely to be a problem in a deregulated, market-driven television industry.

It is a fact of life that a television signal does not recognize national frontiers, and another that in no country in the world has deregulation led to higher standards in programme-making. While working in Rome a few years ago I glimpsed the infamous 'stripping housewives' programme on Signor Berlusconi's channel. It was degrading, disgusting and inexcusable on any grounds whatsoever: but doing the dirty on sex is one of the logical conclusions of grovelling to the market forces. It degrades performer and audience alike.

Ultimately, we have to decide, as citizens, what we think television is for. Perversely, most grown-up writers still see it as a unique and extraordinary medium wherein to celebrate the wonderful diversity of the human spirit, including the spirit of physical love. This is a self-evident truth in all drama from Aristophanes to Arthur Miller. We have earned the right to continue the celebration.

An analysis of sexual activity on the small screen

or The Tufty Club on TV

by Sandi Toksvig

My daughter is a writer', my mother announced confidently over the melon balls at her select gathering of European Women for the Promotion of Conservative Ideals as I passed by with a cold Budweiser up my jumper.

'How fascinating', oozed Madame Petitchou, vice-chair with special responsibility for the emancipation of working women and the proper placement of table decor, 'What are you writing at the moment?'

'It's just something for the uhm...' droplets of ice slid from the cold beer down my stomach, '... the uhm, Broadcasting Standards Council.'

'Standards', my mother echoed, nodding round the table for approval as she expertly slid the sherry decanter over an unfortunate spillage on the table-cloth.

'What is it about?' Frau Apfeltorte asked quietly, mindful of her new burden of representing East and West and the uneasy passage of fashion in a Lada driven economy.

The eyes of Europe were upon me. 'Sex. It's about sex. People having sex on the tele.'

It is not what my mother expected from the Broadcasting Standards Council. Indeed it is not what I expected. Insofar as it had crossed my mind, I assumed in general the Council were not really 'for' sex but I did not think they actually wanted anyone to talk about it. My sole experience with this keeper of moral rectitude, was being referred to the Channel 4 Director of Programmes as required by the Council on the grounds of 'decency and taste' for an episode of the Channel 4 comedy-drama *The Big One* which I wrote with my partner, Elly Brewer.

In the episode in question the father of the character played by Mike McShane is coming for a visit from the United States. It transpires that he is a sexologist. A leading world expert on sexual activity and its permutations or, as my character, Deddie

Tobert, put it 'shagging'. Were we going up the back passage of comedy to smut, just to get a cheap laugh? Well, not just for that.

The gentle Romance novelist, James Howard, we had created for Mike needed an interesting family background to explain such a soft and romantic attitude to life. What better than to make him a rebel?

In one speech he explained – 'My father wanted us to be relaxed about our bodies and other people's for that matter, so there were phalluses all over the house. One year his department gave him a wooden coat rack with four erect penises for our coats and a mahogany vagina on the end to put the car keys in. Let me tell you, when you have hung your hat on a hard-on all your life it gives you kind of an attitude.'

The father then turns up with the coat rack as a gift. It is wrapped in brown paper and never opened but the shape was very clear. (Our assistant designer, Mark, had endless trouble getting the key holder right.) Did this cause offence? A little probably but this was not apparently the 'big issue'. The real subject matter was a line issued by the father in the second half. 'I have a six and a half inch penis when fully erect', he shouted for reasons which seem less clear now that the matter is taken out and waved about on its own (as it were). Here we have the crux of possible offensiveness. It is not that men have penises or women have vaginas that is the problem as long as they lie quietly and do not have a life of their own. Let the organs pump up and be counted, however, then we are all in trouble. Someone's father may have a penis, even a big penis, but it must never, never be 'fully erect'. As for women having clitorises, well, you had just better forget that entirely.

(No one even raised the fact that I had said James made me 'damp in my tufty club', but then as it related to female sexual feelings perhaps no one knew what I was referring to.)

If the actual organs in question are taboo, what are we reduced to with regard to sex on the television? If we are going to have humping on the tele what are we getting for our money? You cannot show the male business other than in its most common, flaccid state and then usually only fleetingly as the actor moves to strategically place a coffee cup in the way. Does this seem too exciting for us all? Well, certainly it would be more thrilling if the man actually balanced the cup on the end of his member.

Men's bottoms seem quite acceptable especially if it is set in Victorian times, he is a bit of a rake and just off for a swim. Women's bottoms are fine but never the 'front bottom'. There is quite a lot of activity around the breasts with the occasional breath-taking close-up of a nipple. Mostly the women lie 'spent' with a sheet draped between their legs which, as any woman can tell you, will leave very awkward stains.

If we do not see much of the couple apart what do we actually see when they get down to it? Certainly a lot of the shots will be of 'his' back as most television lovers are distinctly unoriginal in their choice of final position. The rest of the story may deal with these people as great explorers, outstanding politicians or charismatic movie stars but at the end of the day she still lies down and looks at the ceiling while he pounds away on top. This gives ample time to the contemplation of whether or not a hairy back really does come under the heading of 'exciting'. Occasionally there are supposedly titilating shots from the side with the lovers moulded together. These shots are less enthralling if you think about the fact that these are, after all, actors just doing a day's work which leads one to wonder, if they are not actually 'at it' what is he doing with his dangly business?

One actor told me he always wears a leather thong in intimate scenes. What effect does this have on his partner? Can the actress in question claim professional compensation for the fact that she has chafed one thigh rather badly after a day of dry-humping a goat skin salami under a panoply of 10k lamps?

Tongues are occasionally allowed to make a cameo appearance if the couple are really wild. These are mainly used in scenes to show the person was (a) driven, (b) homosexual and/or (c) a minor, neglected author. The scenes are always well lit and the discarded clothes expensive so that the more prudish audience members have something else to look at if it gets too thrilling. Long established couples and people who live on estates never use tongues. (My one and only screen kiss with Mr McShane was a subject of some tenseness with regard to the tongue but only because he threatened to pass me an anchovy with it during the take.)

That is what we see but what do we hear? This is where we enter into what I consider to be the entirely unexplored world of the sound effect. I once saw a film where a couple were ruffling each other's tufty clubs like mad in a wild frenzy of sexual activity. All standard stuff except the director had decided to use all the natural sounds which emanate from this vigorous activity. There were no wafts of Mozart or busy city sounds to smooth over what is basically a lot of sucking and gurgling noises. Let us pull back the covers and be frank here. Sex is about moistness and moistness creates a world of sound which you may not wish to hear in your living room. I have no doubts that his particular independent film is one which will never make its way on to the small screen. People want passion, not sounds of plumbing in distress.

So if we do not see much and hear even less, what is it all for? If I follow the ads correctly then it seems that sex is there because it sells. The promotion of the new BBC soap *Eldorado* promised us 'Sun, sand, Sangria and of course ... sex'. Why 'of course' sex?

My experience of the sun and Sangria combination ends only in the 'S' word 'sleep' but this is not the real world. This is an artificially created Spanish village where the residents can bonk away out of all proportion and into our living rooms. As we sit sucking the frozen bits in the middle of our microwaved pastie, it is sex we will be told we are longing for and turning on for. Michael Grade, the man who knows about television, says *Eldorado* will be a success because the BBC have spent ten million pounds on something 'sexy'. *Camomile Lawn* was packed with actors having rumpy tumpy. An adaptation of a novel in which the author, as I recall, never found it necessary to actually follow her characters into their bedrooms.

Sex scenes often seem added merely to give additional spice to an otherwise dreary drama. If the people are having sex, they must be interesting. The British have, after all, a long tradition of being simultaneously fascinated and repelled by the physical. It is the land of the hearty back slap, not the double kiss on the cheek. So the question is, what is the harm in it all? Why should the Broadcasting Standards Council be poking their nose in other people's linen.

Why not let the actors who want to ('I felt it was necessary for the part') strip off and get down to it? Let us not just say Mike's father has a fully erect penis, let us see it. Every television comes with an 'off' button.

The trouble is the television image remains a very powerful force. The sexual act between lovers should be the most intimate exchange of affection possible yet the moment the television camera intrudes, the couple are no longer alone. They are in the presence of voyeurs, the audience at home on their Draylon couches. In the novel, we can occupy the inner world of the participants, on television we can only watch. There are not many directors and writers who can and do take the care necessary to portray this intimacy in a positive way.

Too often the sexual act becomes an image of power and, in the exercise of that power, the degradation of one or more of the people involved. I do not mind how many willies or fannies or breasts or tongues we see but I do mind how people are portrayed in their use. For me, watching rape occur is never an artistic statement – it is always about the subjugation of women. It is rare to see a successful, equal and caring relationship portrayed at a time when every lover, whatever their personal predilection, should be thinking very carefully about who they are rubbing bits with.

There are also strange moral codes about what is acceptable. With *Oranges are not the Only Fruit* and *Portrait of a Marriage* there were positive steps towards accepting lesbian love scenes on television. In the latter story, however, of the marriage of Vita and Harold Nicholson, he too had homosexual experiences which were pivotal to their relationship. I do not remember seeing those. We heard about them but there was none of the softly-lit, lace-draped panting that was shown with the women. Are images of women making love more acceptable than a male image of the same thing? Or is it that male television executives merely find the one titillating and the other disturbing? If there is a moral code for broadcasting standards shouldn't we make sure it is the same for everyone? When Colin and Barry hugged on *EastEnders* there was a furore. When Vita kissed Violet we got fashion spreads in the Sunday glossies.

It would be interesting to see if there is a statistical difference between male and female viewers' attitudes to watching sexual activity on the small screen. If book sales are anything to go by then my guess would be that women are more interested in watching romance than actual shagging. It is the moments leading up to intimacy rather than the intimacy which attracts. As a market researcher told me of girls with their Barbie dolls – 'They all want to play at the wedding but none of them want to go on the honeymoon.'

If that is true then it is a worrying thought that sexual images presented on television may be those which are in general acceptable to men. It is rare, for example, to see a sexually voracious woman portrayed as anything other than a figure of fun. A man may still occupy the role of lothario while on-screen women remain either passive or sluts.

(I'm sure there will be statistics gathered for this research. It is an interesting thought that someone will have been employed by the Council to count the number of body parts and their activity in one year's television – Penises 7, Breasts 36, Bottoms (female)

42, Bottoms (male) 3 etc. How do you get a job like that and how do you tell your mother?)

Whatever images presented, does everything, even comedy, need sex to make it sell? I do not think so. Mike McShane and I are living proof that sexual allure need not be a vital ingredient in getting on screen. I may see myself as a sex object but that is only because most people object to having sex with me. I think it is insulting to an audience that a few body parts in grinding motion will be more intriguing than a cracking plot or some sparkling dialogue but I do not suppose that anything will change. I recently received an unsolicited video through the post called *The Lover's Guide II* subtitled 'Making Sex Even Better'. Under its plastic sheath, the tape claimed to provide me with the complete ammunition for 'Sex, desire and communication, planning erotic times together, prolonging foreplay, advanced foreplay, sex games and sex beyond the bedroom', all on my own television. This was everything the broadcasters did not let us see. I was requested to give my comments. Why anyone would want my opinion was unclear to me. You might as well ask Mother Theresa to review *The Hitman and Her*. Still I had a free moment. I do not know if you have ever tried to get the plastic wrapping off a new video. I ended up collapsed on the floor, sweating, and out of breath. Come to think of it, it was the most exciting ten minutes I have had in ages.

Homosexuals and television

by David Morrison

To understand how homosexuals wish to be portrayed by television it is necessary to first understand not just the world the homosexual inhabits, but also to have some understanding about how identity in general is formed and maintained. Indeed, it is by understanding the social process of identity formation that one can see why homosexuals are concerned about how television presents them.

The idea of self

The establishment of identity is a continual and continuous process. It is not a question, as with popular mystical ideas, of finding the 'true' self, but of establishing a boundary of meaning which includes a recognition of one's own place and persona. This is not done alone. And because it is not done alone, it is now within the individual's capacity to control entirely. The meanings which one establishes that allow the development of the feeling of separateness from others – the uniqueness of personality – are constructed in association with others. Yet the 'others' of this collective enterprise are no more in control of the conditions of their development than anyone else. This area of control, or power, we may call culture, which – while created by individuals – does not bear the mark of any single individual.

Indeed, as a collective enterprise, culture represents not only the meanings that individuals have formed in the present about the world, but those meanings that have been fashioned in the past and carried over or re-worked to become part of the sediment of existing culture. Culture, therefore, stands as an external force to the individual, at times clearly recognisable and at times not so recognisable.

But for any belief system to be strong or practices accepted as legitimate, the plausibility structures surrounding beliefs or practices must be strong. However the plausibility structures surrounding the belief that homosexuality is a legitimate way to express human sexuality are weak. For this very reason – that their form of sexuality is not reflected in the symbolic universe of the everyday presentation of sex – the homosexual has to build his or her own structure of legitimation. But, to have to make and remake one's own definitions of self on a virtually continuous basis is exhausting and also, it must be added, a fragile exercise. Indeed, psychological security cannot be maintained on an individual basis. Such stability is assured only by being anchored in a system of shared understandings. Once we understand this, we can understand homosexuals' sensitivity about how their sexuality is portrayed on television.

The life world of the homosexual

Although heterosexuals may have sexual predilections that they might be reluctant to broadcast, no heterosexual in our society need fear the exposure that he or she is attracted to the opposite member of his or her sex. To be sexually attracted to the opposite sex is taken to be normal; indeed, it is assumed that members of the opposite sex will be attracted to each other and often precautions are taken to separate the sexes in situations where sexual attraction is not socially desired. Thus, no heterosexual has to feel embarrassed, guilty or defensive about his or her sexuality. The homosexual, on the other hand, lives, to varying degrees, in a hostile world. And it is this hostile world, unimaginable to the heterosexual, that shapes the homosexual's response to the portrayal of sex on television. Thus, let us first look at the manner in which the homosexual has to negotiate his or her sexuality.

All the homosexuals that were talked to in the groups defined their own sexuality as 'normal'. The most commonly used word to describe their own behaviour, and indeed that of anyone else, was 'natural'. Providing the participants had consented or were capable of consent, they saw sex as natural (no matter what the variations of performance it might include) and therefore a legitimate expression of human sexual ambition. They were not about to proscribe certain sexual behaviour because they were only too well aware of their place as proscribed sexual types. The one word that stung them more than anything else was that of 'pervert'; they saw themselves as normal. However, to see oneself as normal does not alter the response of others who do not share that view. Thus, a great deal of effort had to be placed on the presentation of the self.

For example, asked if people at work knew she was a lesbian, one woman in London commented that it was the 'situation (that) dictates whether or not you are going to make yourself vulnerable. She complained that no one would dream of asking someone if they were heterosexual, but what is important is the fact that she used the term 'vulnerable' to describe her response to questions about her sexuality. It is here that we come back to the idea of identity. To have to keep secret a vital part of one's self is not simply a strain of the type that, say, a spy might face, but threatens the very idea of self; a denial of an essential part of one's existence. Male homosexuals at times deliberately hid the fact that they were homosexuals in those situations where they felt not to do so would be physically dangerous, most usually late at night in places where heterosexuals were gathered. Some of the male homosexuals had been beaten up and saw fit to mention that men had been killed because they were gay.

Some of the experiences related in the groups, but particularly by the women, were sad indeed. What we are talking about here, however, is not sex, but the pain that flowed from an individual's sexuality that restricted affection from sources where one might normally expect it to be given. A lesbian couple from Oldham had a particularly difficult time from the family of the younger one in the relationship:

> 'I got called a few names because I am the older one in the relationship – it was
> my fault. As far as her family is concerned when she sorts herself out she will

become normal. Her mum was very bad. I got called everything under the sun. Very upsetting for the both of us. I cried a few times.'

To accept the idea that one is not normal in the context of something that is seen as normal – sex – is difficult to accept. And of course, the homosexuals interviewed refused such labelling. But they had to constantly struggle against definitions which, if accepted, would cast them into the nether reaches of humanity. In this respect the women appeared, at least in emotional terms, to be presented with a much more difficult time than male homosexuals. It was much more difficult for them to accept a self-definition of themselves as homosexuals. One woman said she felt 'shame' on realizing that she was a lesbian: 'I gave myself a hard time really about it. At that time I was very young. I was coming to terms with my sexuality'. Another woman said that she used to deny that she was a lesbian, and said that 'I feel quite angry enough now not to and be proud and strong and feel OK.' However, the protection of the self was not complete: 'I disguise it sometimes, if I don't feel safe. I am wary of attitudes around me and I do not want ... to put myself in a vulnerable position'.

One of the problems for female homosexuals in creating a territory of acceptance is that heterosexual men find it difficult to accept lesbianism as a preferred sexual state. Homosexuality in women was seen as of doubtful authenticity. One woman said a basic reaction of men was, 'you have not met the right man yet, and let me take you home and you won't want to sleep with another women after you have had me'.

This refusal to accept lesbianism did make for special difficulties for the women in a way not experienced by the men.

The women felt that their femininity was under attack because they were lesbians. By and large the men did not feel that their masculinity was under attack because they were homosexuals – although the men often faced hostility and ridicule, at least they had the benefit of knowing that their sexual status was recognized.

Both men and women found it distressing that they could not show their feelings in public towards those of the same sex that they were fond of. Rights that were accorded heterosexuals were denied them. They felt emotionally disenfranchized. One quote will capture the sense of emotional impoverishment that at times homosexuals must accept.

> 'We had a dinner (in a restaurant) some time ago and it would have been really nice to sort of actually hold hands and sort of be close as other heterosexual couples. Yet we couldn't. We would probably have got disapproving glances from everybody. I mean when you are walking in the countryside in Derby-shire and you are feeling good but you can't express that feeling of goodness and happiness with your partner. That is difficult, and I am not sure how that fits in with being lonely, but there is something missing there.'

A place in the sun

What homosexuals want is to be accepted for what they are: individuals like everyone else, but who happen to find the object of their sexual desires focus on members of their own sex rather than the opposite sex. They wanted their sexuality to stop being seen as a problem. For them, it was not a problem, but, as discussed in the opening section, a sense of identity is not built alone, but in association with others. And the others in the collective activity of identity-building refused to see homosexuality as a legitimate expression of sexuality. Thus the homosexuals had to constantly defend their own idea of the self, and fight off counter definitions of correct sexual identity.

One response, and common to any 'out' group, was to create enclosed worlds where the plausibility structures of homosexuality as a legitimate expression of the sexual self could remain intact. This option appeared more readily available to the men than the women, but the simple fact is that the enclosed world was usually that of the homosexual club or pub which could not act as a total fortress against the outside world of heterosexual beliefs about sexuality.

By and large, therefore, the response of homosexuals to the position that they found themselves in was not that of retreatism, but a desire that the dominant culture would change, and in doing so encompass homosexuality as part of the natural order of things. What they wanted was for people to view homosexuality as a point or place on a continuum of sexual being. But if this was not possible then they wanted people at least not to view homosexuals as odd. That is, if the heterosexual community could not accept homosexuality as a legitimate expression of sexuality, then the very least it could do was not place the homosexual's sexuality in the foreground as if that was the most significant feature of their personality. If, in other words, heterosexuals could not accept homosexuality as sexual behaviour, then what the heterosexual community could do was to accept the homosexual as an individual with talents, ambitions and hopes in the same way that they might accept anyone else.

These twin hopes or demands framed the homosexuals' response to the portrayal of sexuality on television. On the one hand they wished for television to portray homosexuals in their full capacity as human beings, which necessarily included them as having sexual desires and a sex life, and on the other hand they wanted homosexuals to occupy character roles, where although their sexuality was known, this did not affect their performance.

These twin demands come together in one ultimate demand – the normalization of homosexuals in society. This is what they wanted from television. As one woman said:

> 'Lesbians are a way of life anyway and it is silly that they are not present in the soap opera or anything. It would be interesting too for people to get to know a character in a soap before they came out as a lesbian – lesbians work in cafes and do this and that you know.'

The above is a good example of the desire for the normalization of homosexuality through the portrayal of homosexuals as normal people. And the way television could do that, as the above comment indicates, is to show the homosexual as mundane rather than as special. One man was even more insistent that television should feature the homosexual as person, rather than the person as homosexual:

> 'I am fed up actually with homosexuals being on television just to address the issue of homosexuality. There are no homosexual doctors who are there because they have a doctor in a story.'

This normalization of homosexuality through the mundane presentation of homosexuals was something that most men and women in the groups thought television could readily achieve. However, as part of the normalization process they still wanted homosexuality as sexual behaviour to be presented, and on the same terms that heterosexual behaviour was. To do so, they thought, would be beneficial. As one man said:

> 'I would like to see a little bit more (homosexual sex), maybe not for my sake but for the benefit of young people. I am still angry that I did not have any role models when I was young that would have made my life a lot easier. I feel strongly about that.'

Neither he, nor other homosexuals, considered it likely, at least at the moment, for television to give much support to normalization through the portrayal of homosexual sex.

The position of some members of the groups was that a heterosexually-dominated culture that does not, or cannot, portray heterosexuality openly is hardly likely to advance the portrayal of homosexuality. The following point was made by a man:

> 'I suppose that possibly as a society we are more prudish about sex (than the rest of Europe) and really I feel we ought not to be. There are so many taboos and it sort of reflects on our attitude to homosexuality as well as perhaps if we had more sexuality on television then perhaps people would have a more enlightened view or attitude to homosexuality as well'.

Permission to be normal: an end note

We have seen, both theoretically and empirically, the difficulties that homosexuals face in contemporary sexual culture and how they struggle to define their own sexuality as legitimate in the face of hostile definitions of sexuality. The holding together of the personality is a continual and continuous task, and as stated, is done in conjunction with the surrounding world of others. But part of that surrounding world is television. The images that are portrayed are carried, although in mediated form, into the everyday world of understandings. What homosexuals wished from television is that it should help them, in their everyday life, to present the self in a way that they would like. They wished to establish for themselves a sense of identity not infected by the imposition of ideas from the heterosexual world that distorted who or what they were. As one man remarked:

> 'The point I would like to make really is that we sort of homed in on how you portrayed gay sex. I just want to go back to the simple fact that I want the whole cultural society to represent my lifestyle alongside other people's lifestyles as perfectly normal'.

Sexual standards

by Cate Haste

When we were making one of the early Channel 4 documentary series in 1984 about sex, *Just Sex*, our aim was to explore changing attitudes through two groups, one all women, one all men, who broadly reflected a range of different classes, ages, religions, races and sexual orientations. We pre-interviewed a very large number of people, often in groups. The centrepiece of each programme was to be a two day discussion covering the themes of all the programmes, and we then drew on visual material from films, television, magazines etc. to illustrate the changes. The age range – from 25 to 82 – meant the participants would implicitly reflect the changes of almost a century.

It was immediately clear that we had to adopt an entirely different approach for those aged over 50–55 from those younger. Asking younger people to take part in programmes on 'sex' was no problem. Under 25 they were unstoppable. However the word 'sex' was off-putting to older people. Though they were quite happy to talk about 'courtship, marriage and morals' they felt able to discuss more 'intimate' topics only after their confidence in us had been established. It was the use of terms which mattered; we had to circumnavigate euphemisms before we found they were just as willing to talk honestly about their personal experience of, and attitudes to, sex and relationships.

The generation divide has been of key significance in nearly three decades of rapidly changing sexual values. On almost all the main moral shifts – pre-marital sex, cohabitation, freedom of expression or censorship – the over-50s take a more conservative attitude, to the extent that polls routinely point out the gap between responses of different age groups because they differ so starkly (and so skew the averages). This discrepancy appears as well in the Broadcasting Standards Council's survey, which shows a higher proportion of those who are anti-sex on television in this age group than in any other. Any comedy producer who defends his programmes by saying they are not intended for anyone over the age of 35 acknowledges the divide.

The language and vocabulary of sex have changed fundamentally, and the cusp of that change was the 1960s. For most people brought up before then, sex was private, and the public code was one of restraint bordering on taboo. Since then, sex has become a proper subject for representation, imaginative depiction and examination at every level of public discourse.

We decided at the outset of the series that no subject was taboo. We were asking people to talk conversationally about their experiences. The fact that 25 to 40 year olds were at ease with explicit words – 'fuck', 'orgasm', 'vagina', 'penis' – but older members of the group might not be was in itself revealing. The group dynamic meant they sorted out the vocabulary and to some extent the subject matter themselves, using language they thought appropriate to the setting.

The only controversy came over the programme *Sex for Sale* dealing with prostitution and pornography. I had included an extract from a Canadian film *Not a Love Story* – a verité scene, with natural sound and conversation, of a stills shoot for a porn magazine. The participants were elaborately rigged out in pirate costumes, with several women in flowing skirts and a man wearing a patch, a sword and full silk scarf round his waist trailing over his thighs. The conversation consisted of a woman in an awkward pose which occasionally revealed her genitals complaining of discomfort and the man at one point laconically asking, 'Do you want the dick in (picture)?' Said dick was of singular proportions, though not erect and just about visible among the scarf's folds.

I had already placed a caption super over the most explicit parts but Channel 4 wanted the scene cut. This raised certain important issues. The scene was included because it showed the fantasy of pornography, and the utter banality of its making. I thought it was tasteful, given the subject, and there were no close-ups. In its context I also thought the whole thing was hilarious, so it was an important change of mood. But most important it raised the question of how can you deal with visual pornography if you don't illustrate it? It would be misleading to restrict the visual images to soft-focus soft porn if we know it is much more than that, and often nastier.

Eventually we kept the scene but cut off the lower 23 per cent of the screen to delete the potentially offensive part. Which part was offensive was never made clear. Female genitalia, the stock in trade of 'soft' porn at the time, had apparently never been shown on television, and there has always been a ban on the erect penis. But we wondered whether the non-erect penis, which had provoked much astonished comment from men, was the more offending member. Men seem more sensitive about representations of their 'private parts' than of women's.

The series reflected the age. It has become as acceptable for broadcasters to tackle sex as openly as any other subject of public and private interest. And rightly so, since it is central to most people's lives, a constant inspiration for comedians, dramatists, novelists, and the grist to public and political debate ranging through AIDS, rape, and sexual abuse to divorce and privacy legislation. Apart from this, as J. B. Priestley pointed out during an earlier controversy over literature, it is misleading to suppose sex can only be discovered in print or on television for 'there is so much sex in most people's heads that a writer would have to work very hard to put any more in it'.

The broadcasting authorities have reflected changes in society's moral attitudes. Since the early 60s they steadily divested themselves of their former role as the guardians of public morality. The shift came when the BBC under its Director General, Sir Hugh

Greene, responded to the perceived breakup of the moral consensus by replacing its Reithian commitment to elevate audience tastes with a pluralistic policy which he thought befitted a morally pluralistic society. The BBC's aim, Greene said, was to mirror society, inquire and challenge accepted views, and recognize an obligation towards tolerance and maximum liberty of expression. What mattered was the treatment of the subject, its relevance to the audience and the tide of opinion in society; though 'outrage was impermissible', shock was not always so, and 'provocation may be healthy and indeed socially imperative'.

These guidelines have not in essence changed. Within their Charter and Statute obligations not to include anything 'offensive to public feeling' or which 'offends against good taste or decency', the broadcasters have engaged in almost permanent debate about the limits of tolerance and freedom of expression. Meanwhile, the definitions of what is bad taste or offensive have shifted constantly.

The broadcasting authorities have generally taken into account those vociferous groups whose view of broadcasting's role differed fundamentally from that of broad-casters. Mary Whitehouse believed its role was to uphold Christian standards, whereas broadcasters saw it as mirroring a pluralistic society, encouraging under-standing of differing viewpoints. She saw sex as private, and sexual representations as intrusions into that privacy, whereas in society in general it became increasingly public. While broadcasters were extending the imaginative range of their work and addressing the complexities of love and sexual relations with greater frankness, the puritan lobby wanted to rein them in to the confines of what seemed to broadcasters a narrow interpretation of the Christian ethic.

This lobby tapped a more general anxiety and confusion about rapidly changing values and the loss of a firm moral purpose, but it also helped shape an atmosphere of panic about 'excessive' sex on television. This was sustained through much of the seventies and eighties. It acquired political weight within the framework of the Conservative Party's commitment in the early eighties to a return to Victorian values and its use of the rhetoric of anti-permissiveness in support of 'traditional family values'.

However during the eighties, people's behaviour and attitudes moved further away from the 'traditional' moral code and became more libertarian. Pre-marital sex in-creased, cohabitation became more widespread, few people married, more children were born outside marriage, divorce continued to increase and the number of one-parent families rose. The exception to this trend was a reversal of liberal attitudes to homosexuality and an increase in homophobia as a result probably of the AIDS issue and Clause 28 legislation. Otherwise there are few signs that we are returning to a more puritan moral climate.

Whether there is a difference between people's behaviour, and their attitudes towards the representation of sex on television remains an open question. Clearly the context of television viewing makes a difference. I am probably not alone in switching off television when something was on which I thought unsuitable – because too 'adult' – for my young children, though not unsuitable for myself to watch. I may in the company of older people have been inclined to switch away from something which I thought they might feel uncomfortable about watching when I was there. But this does not mean that such programmes should not be on the screen; I would watch them in the company of peers.

It is arguable whether there has ever been 'too much' sex on television. During a period of unaccustomed freedom in the 1970s when some broadcasters, along with dramatists, novelists and comedians, felt a sense of crusade about testing and pushing back frontiers and breaking down taboos, the balance between considerations of context, audience sensitivity and treatment of sex became more fluid. Now, in a possibly more sexually educated, aware and even mature society, the crusading spirit of frankness or shock for its own sake is hardly evident. Sex is invariably portrayed in context, virtually never gratuitous, and not very often explicit. It is fenced off by the Watershed and signposted with warnings where this is considered appropriate.

If broadcasters are to continue to reflect the society in which they operate, with a duty to enlarge understanding as well as to entertain and inform, then confronting the dilemmas and delights of the most profound emotional experiences in life – love, sex, marriage/partnerships – as well as acknowledging the diversity and variety of sexual and emotional behaviour is an essential part of their role. The same rigorous standards as apply to other areas of public service broadcasting – the search for truth, the challenge to accepted opinions and passing fashions, the fair representation of a diversity of views and experiences, and the imaginative exploration of human experience also apply to the treatment of sex.

And sex is regularly a central issue in public debate. Broadcasters have a responsibility to reflect that over the range of programming. AIDS has preoccupied health educators and the public for almost a decade, generated controversy about moral and sexual behaviour, and contributed to a major shift away from tolerance towards homophobia. This has produced a vociferous response from gays, not least about their representation in the media. Sexual abuse has equally generated shock and fierce public debate. Feminists have challenged society's assumptions about female sexuality, which has led to some changes in the way women are portrayed in the media, and contributed to a more realistic representation of women's sexual lives.

Because we are also in an age of moral confusion without a monolithic code, there is a need to explore moral and sexual issues in the context of diversity and tolerance, rather than in an atmosphere of repression and censorship. This puts a responsibility on broadcasters to make programmes which aim to clarify, enlarge understanding, and explore honestly the sexual undercurrents of the society in which we live.

However, the product of anxiety about 'too much' sex on television has been a proliferation of controls which include the BBC's regulatory machinery, the new Independent Television Commission, the Broadcasting Standards Council and the extension of the Obscene Publications Acts to cover broadcasting. While these function to regulate as well as provide a conduit for public protest, they also carry with them the danger that broadcasters may become more timid and self censoring, and the programmes more bland in the face of possible hostility. 'Even directors of programmes get fed up with the hassle and start dreaming of interviews by Jimmy Young instead of a constant hail of sandbags. Is this what the public really wants?' Liz Forgan, deputy head of Channel 4, asked recently.

Paradoxically this has occurred at a time when the government's aim has been to demolish the existing monopoly structure of broadcasting and encourage market competition and a proliferation of outlets. Yet this is likely to make it more, not less, difficult to control programme content. With increased competition and scarce resources, the fear of those reared in the public service ethic is that audience ratings will figure even more prominently in decisions and that this will inevitably lower rather than raise programme standards.

If one is to draw any conclusions from the fiercely competitive climate of the newspaper industry, it is that editors know that sex and scandal sell newspapers. The quality papers are beginning to follow the tabloids in their reliance on sexual stories up to their market share. I know of no broadcaster who has included sex in a programme because it will increase audience ratings. But, with increased competition, the decline of the public service ethos in broadcasting and the difficulty of controlling outlets, it is not difficult to foresee a time when sex acquires a much more commercial value on the screen. Nor is it difficult to see that certain broadcasters will take note and act accordingly. I doubt that this is what the government or the regulators intended.

Sex on French television

by François Hurard

In a country which has inherited a tradition of courtly love, lauded by its earliest poets and troubadours who knew how to combine the sense of moral rigour that Jansenism had and the tendency towards frivolity displayed in art (the colour of flesh in Poussin; Fragonard's nudes; Diderot's 'indiscreet' eroticism in his writings ...), it is surprising that, in this modern age, television has not recognized its cultural heritage earlier and has ignored Eros.

However it is only recently that French television has allowed eroticism and sexuality on to its screens.

In fact, until 1985–86 (when the commercial channels were launched), the monopoly of public service broadcasting on all three publicly-available television channels was the guarantor or guardian of 'good behaviour' on the small screen.

Public broadcasting had a triple mission – 'to inform, educate and entertain', but neither sex education (introduced in schools in 1974) nor, even less, the depiction of erotica had their place in its programming. It was risky for a television producer to linger on the body of an actress, and even less advisable for him to show the carnal nature of a relationship between fictional characters, except as a brief shot or with appropriate lighting. The famous 'white square' warned parents of the risqué content of a programme, but even this fell under strict conditions.

Yet there was no internal code, no practical guide for producers which warned of the taboos and banned camera angles. It was left to them to practise self-censorship, and to each channel's programme controller to exercise an absolute decision as to what limits were acceptable.[8]

During the seventies, at that time today called – with the dead-pan expression of the historian – 'the sexual revolution', a good many areas of society were affected. With *Emmanuelle* (1973) and *The Story of O* (1975), the cinema had experienced a new vogue, that of eroticism, tapping a large audience and Parliament in France soon had to

---

8 Only a short note was included in the specifications for the three channels which reminded directors to see that their programmes 'comply with the laws and statutory provisions on good moral standards and public morality'.

intervene to legislate on 'hard' pornographic films (the 1974 law on the X rating). In the press world, the so-called 'girlie' magazines (based on *Playboy*, the one which led the way), mushroomed and their sales soared. Finally, the video was shortly to make its appearance and see its market expand, in the initial stages, through the circulation of erotic and pornographic films.

Television, a medium for the masses, and the object of family entertainment par excellence for that very reason, was to remain unreceptive to these trends and was to resist the temptations of the flesh for several years. Then, in the mid-eighties, a decisive step was taken.

The channels that changed it all

From 1985, one of the three state channels, FR3, created a slot for showing films which were forbidden to under-age viewers: *Last Tango in Paris* and *The Night Porter*. That same year saw the launch of the first private channel: Canal Plus. Since this encrypted channel operated on the subscription principle, it devoted most of its broadcasting time to cinema. It naturally offered films to its public which had never before been shown on television, particularly genre films (horror, martial arts, soft porn). On 31 August 1985, less than a month after its launch, Canal Plus broadcast the first X-rated film[9] – never seen previously on television. This was to become a regular feature, with one X film per month being repeated three times between midnight and five o'clock in the morning, available in decoded form to subscribers only.[10]

However, this programming provoked little reaction from the public.[11]

In actual fact, the genuine innovation came from the state channel, Antenne 2, and its magazine programme, *Sexy Follies*, which was broadcast for the first time in April 1986. It was to set a tone of light eroticism on television, one which was suitable for a wider audience rather than for only aficionados of the genre. Shown at 10.30 pm and consisting of short sequences (striptease, celebrity interviews, features, advice), this magazine programme distilled a very civilized eroticism in measured doses: artistic nudity, a very intellectual and metaphorical voyeurism, in short, a lot more talk than naked bodies. In other words, the opposite to pornographic realism ... .

The formula was to be adopted a year later by TF1 which, however, abandoned it shortly afterwards. Nevertheless, it was to inspire countless other magazine programmes of a similar type. As described below, the private channel, M6, has come to specialize in such programming.

Finally, in 1986, FR3 (the third state channel) launched itself into erotic fiction with adaptations of erotic works of French literature (the *Série Rose* or 'Pink Series'), which were broadcast after midnight on Saturdays.

---

9   The X rating indicates that unsimulated sex acts are shown.

10 The emergence of sex on television is, therefore, interrelated in historical terms with the development of commercial television. And it is alarming to note that this intrusion was made straight away in the most extreme form, that of pornography.

11 It is true that it only involved a limited number of subscribers, a few hundred thousand at the time, while today 3.3 million homes subscribe to Canal Plus.

The two new private channels which emerged in 1987 (La Cinq and M6) likewise were to exploit eroticism as a special niche with a boldness that was intensified by their status as commercial channels. From 1988 onwards, La Cinq was to introduce the sustained programming of erotic (soft porn) films. At the same time, M6 set in motion the production of erotic magazine programmes and imitated La Cinq in the scheduling of films. Today it is the only channel to broadcast such material every weekend after 11.00 pm (*Sexy-Clip*, *Charmes*, and *Vénus*).

Today, television's craze for this type of programme has returned to more reasonable levels. The state channels (Antenne 2 and FR3) have become unsullied again (a way of distinguishing themselves from the commercial channels) while TF1, a private channel which in itself attracts more than 40 per cent of the audience, also behaves more judiciously. This leaves the privilege of broadcasting such programming to M6 and Canal Plus, channels with more limited audiences.

The ethics of the public broadcasting channels and TF1, which aim to attract a very wide audience, got the better of eroticism to which they had resorted in the early stages of the end of the state monopoly. This is seen by the distinction that has been made between general or 'popular' programming (offered by these channels) and programming that may be called specialist or intended solely for adults.

Television's discovery of sexuality

The vogue of 'reality television', which appeared at the end of the eighties, made television the omnipresent witness to social trends, and the lives of individuals. As the cameras forgot the barriers of discretion and modesty, they wanted to scrutinize the ups and downs of human psychology and cross the frontiers of private life, exposing at random feelings, emotions and passions. These were displayed to the public by a television avid for openness.

It was Antenne 2 that took the first initiative in this area with its magazine programme *Psyshow*, a psychosociological programme with interviews in which individuals explained their problems with their relationships, sometimes going beyond the barriers of decency in their dialogue with the camera. The apotheosis of this genre is certainly the programme, broadcast by TF1 since 1991, *L'amour en danger* where a couple, using reconstruction, discussions and a psycho-dramatic sequence conducted under the supervision of a psychoanalyst, explain their private problems and try to solve them with millions of television viewers looking on.

Exhibitionism or catharsis? The commentators, all critical, have not failed to notice this type of television experiment, which has successfully scaled the heights in terms of audience ratings.

An investigative documentary (*L'amour en France* – 9 episodes of 52 minutes length) shown on Antenne 2 in 1989, looked at the sexuality of the French. It attracted much comment, and criticism, from the Conseil Supérieur de l'Audiovisuel when, in one sequence, a young child was asked to show his private parts to his little classmates.

Health and information magazine programmes also regularly tackle the problems of sexuality – from the medical angle in the case of the former (sex disorders, sexually – transmitted diseases), and from a social angle in the case of the latter (the sex market, prostitution, deviant sexual practices, etc.), usually with an assured success with the audience. At times, though, they have not managed to steer clear of foundering on the reef of voyeurism, albeit intentionally or otherwise, in the guise of informing the public.

Public opinion

Several surveys and opinions polls were carried out in 1988 and 1989, looking at the public's attitude towards sex and violence on television.

An initial examination of the results of these polls reveals a remarkable tolerance by the French public regarding the way in which sexuality is depicted on the small screen. It is particularly noticeable that sex is much more readily accepted than violence.

Yet tolerance is not licence.

Although the majority of the polls reflect the fact that French television viewers are not at all ashamed to state their choices and practise what they preach (as demonstrated by the excellent ratings for some soft porn films or magazine programmes), this tolerance is combined with a very clear, even imperative, perception that there are certain limits or excesses that are not to be over-stepped or breached.[12]

Thus, when, in 1988, an opinion poll (see Table 1) asked viewers to express an opinion about the programming of X-rated films (hard porn) at 8.30 pm on television, the majority said that they were against it (63 per cent).[13]

Another opinion poll, published a few months later, confirmed the choice (by a majority of the French) of a 'Watershed' fixed at around 10.00 pm or 10.30 pm. It also yielded certain interesting facts when it came to those who rejected the idea of total freedom on television. When questioned about soft porn films (Tables 3 and 4), only 28 per cent of respondents declared themselves to be in favour of total freedom compared with 69 per cent who objected to the idea (with 3 per cent don't knows). These objectors could be broken down into three separate groups:

> (a) A group, very much in the minority, advocating a total ban on soft porn films on television (5 per cent of all the people questioned).

---

12 From this point of view, the public's tolerance is very clearly reduced when children are involved. One recent experiment in sex education is a cartoon broadcast by FR3 (entitled 'Le bonheur de la vie' or 'The happiness of living') which aroused a great deal of protest of an ethical or religious nature, despite the care taken by its creators.

13 Women, people over sixty and senior white collar workers were more likely to be against it than men, the 15–24 year olds and workers, which is not really surprising. Bearing in mind the frequent confusion which is made by the majority of the public between 'hard' pornography (X-rated films) and soft porn (films forbidden to the under-sixteens), it is fair to think that this rejection of programming extends to both these categories of films. Furthermore, this confirms an opinion poll carried out in November 1989 (see Table 2) which included a question on the scheduling of erotic films (soft porn): 66% of those questioned disapproved of broadcasting them at 8.30 pm (compared with 25% who declared that they were in favour). On the other hand, 68% approved the showing of soft porn films at 10.00 pm.

(b)   A second group, easily the largest (47 per cent of all those questioned) who were in favour of a 10.30 pm programming slot.

(c)   Finally, a third group which declared themselves in favour of a simple warning (white square) which indicated that the film was for adults only, irrespective of the transmission time (17 per cent of all the people questioned).

Table 1. Are you for or against the showing of X-rated films on television at 8.30 pm?

	For 30%	Against 53%
Men	33%	58%
Women	26%	68%
15–24 year-olds	34%	56%
25–34 year-olds	38%	57%
50–59 year-olds	20%	66%
Those sixty and over	21%	72%
Senior white collar workers	21%	70%
Technicians, clerks, middle management	32%	61%
Workers and labourers	41%	52%
Practising Catholics	24%	70%
Non-practising Catholics	32%	62%
Non-Catholics	30%	57%

A poll of a nationally representative sample of 800 respondents aged 18 and over, carried out by Ipsos and Le Point on 19 November 1988.

Table 2.

In the case of each of the following types of broadcast, would you like the Conseil Supérieur de l'Audiovisuel (CSA) to ban them, ask that they be shown after 10.30 p.m., have them marked with a white square, or allow the channels to decide for themselves?

Soft porn broadcasts like *Super Sexy:*	
Ban them	5%
Show them after 10.30 pm	44%
Mark with white square	12%
Allow the channels to do as they like	36%
Don't knows	3%

Soft porn films like *Emmanuelle:*	
Ban them	5%
Show them after 10.30 pm	47%
Mark with white square	17%
Allow the channels to do as they like	28%
Don't knows	3%

IPSOS opinion poll; February 1989. A nationally representative sample of eight hundred people (aged 18 and over) were questioned by telephone.

Table 3. Do you feel personally that at the present time there are too many or not enough sex scenes on TV?

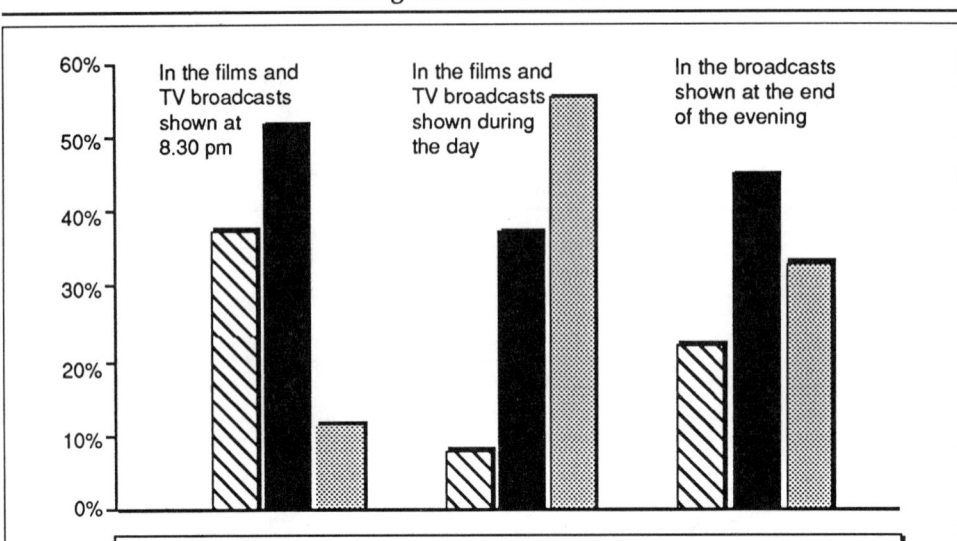

Table 4. Eroticism and the white square. Do you feel personally that at the present time there are too many or not enough sex scenes on TV?

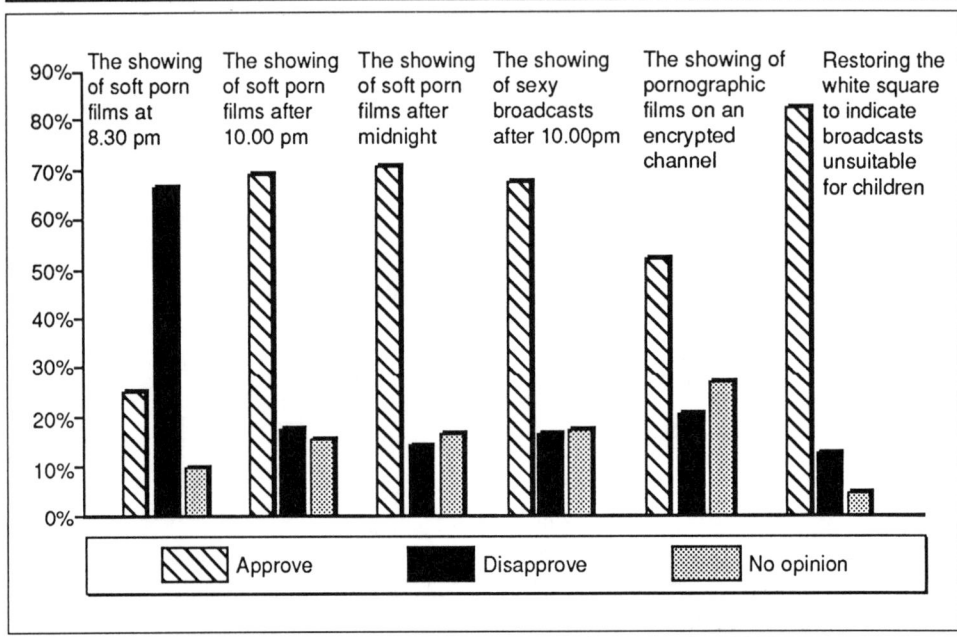

Tables 3 & 4. Opinion poll carried out by phone on 2, 3 and 4 November 1988, on a representative sample of the French population of 907 people of eighteen and over.

A brief glance at the audience ratings for soft porn broadcasts and films, even for those information programmes that tackle subjects connected with sexuality, would quickly show that this topic excites the viewer's curiosity, and confirms the trends outlined in the various opinion polls, mentioned above.

In a system that is largely financed (the state channels) or wholly financed (the private channels) by advertising revenue, this public curiosity has a clear commercial value to the television channels.

The economics of sex on television

At a time when the plentiful supply of low-cost programmes becomes a priority for certain commercial TV channels, and when audience research sometimes leads broadcasters to underestimate certain elementary principles of deontology or ethics, the temptation to show soft porn programmes is often an extremely successful commercial decision, for reasons which are quite simple.

The first is the low cost of soft or hard porn programmes: to give an example, the budget of a hard porn film rarely exceeds FF500,000 whereas the average budget of a film in France is around twenty-five million francs. The same applies to the information magazine programmes or documentaries. The cost/audience ratio of these programmes is therefore clearly advantageous to broadcasters, and the temptation to resort, on a massive scale, to this type of programming is only moderated by the imperatives of respectability which the broadcasters impose on themselves in order to maintain a relationship of trust with the widest possible audience.

La Cinq, which planned in 1988 to show one soft porn film regularly every week, followed an expertly calculated commercial strategy. The supply of soft porn films available on the market at that time was put at about a hundred titles; the majority of these were films banned to the under-twelves, or more commonly, the under-sixteens. Amongst them, the complete series of the *Emmanuelle* films, *The Story of O*, the films of David Hamilton, etc. All of these were acquired at fees a lot lower than the normal purchase prices for full-length feature films.[14]

As the risk of showing such material could not be taken by a channel like TF1 – which aims for a very wide audience – and even less so by the state service for ethical reasons, this programming remained unrivalled. So, the acquisition of the catalogue of soft porn films was facilitated (no other channel really showed any interest in it) and the cost/audience ratio was very good. It was also clear that one section of the viewing public was insatiable for a genre of the cinema's repertoire which, until then, had not had access to the small screen. If this channel, as it wished originally, had shown those films at 8.30 pm, it would have been an extremely fruitful commercial operation.

Regulation swiftly put an end to that attempt, and, by acting in this way, a form of unfair competition was also halted.

---

14 Generally speaking, these films cost less, even a lot less, than one million francs for two showings, compared with two to six million francs for family films that were major box office hits, like *Indiana Jones* , *The Bear*, etc.

The regulator's role

Radio and television regulatory bodies have existed in France since 1982. The first of them was la Haute Autorité de la Communication Audiovisuelle which had not remained blind to the emergence of sex on the small screen. The action they took however, evolved according to applicable laws, and also the practices of the broadcasters. From 1982 to 1986, still operating within a state service monopoly, la Haute Autorité made a judgement about the quality of the programmes shown. It examined, in particular, complaints sent to it by viewers or associations. Despite broadcasts by FR3 of films with erotic overtones from 1984 onwards, and the broadcasting of *Sexy Follies* by Antenne 2, it did not intervene. Instead, in its annual reports published from 1984–86, the Haute Autorité laid special emphasiss on the need to warn the public, in appropriate ways, of the content of certain films which were forbidden viewing for those under-age.

The law on communications was to undergo an upheaval in September 1986, when there was a declaration of 'the freedom of communications'. A new regulatory authority was created, with the power to grant broadcasting licences, to monitor compliance by the services with regard to their programme obligations, and – of particular importance – to punish any abuse of the law, under the guidance of a judge on administrative matters.

It was for the CNCL (Commission Nationale de la Communications et des Libertés), set up in December 1986, to establish a delicate balance between the defence of freedom of expression and the imperative of 'safe-guarding childhood and adolescence' (Article 15 of the law of 1986) which, along with the concept of 'compliance with the dignity of the human being', were the only grounds on which the authorities could intervene over the content of programmes.

The law therefore only laid down very general principles and it was the task of the regulator to interpret, or even to expand on, them. This task of interpretation was, first of all, to be undertaken in a fairly pragmatic way, guided by the law.

From 1987 onwards, the CNCL had to stem the rising tide of 'problem' broadcasts: violent films and television programmes, soft porn programmes, etc.

Its first action of any significance was in 1988 when La Cinq decided to show one soft porn film (banned viewing to the under-twelves or under-sixteens) every Thursday evening at 8.30 pm. After showing two films, banned to the under-twelves, the channel went into a higher gear and announced that it was to show a film forbidden to the under-sixteens, entitled *Joy et Joan* (in which one of the stars of French hard porn cinema, Brigitte Lahaye, appeared). A warning was sent to the channel by the CNCL saying the film should be shown at a later time. La Cinq publicly announced that it was keeping to its programming schedule. In the light of this refusal to comply, the CNCL brought emergency interim proceedings before the judge on administrative matters (the Council of State), who was called upon to issue a ruling on the case before the film was to be shown.

After viewing the film and hearing lawyers for the two parties, the judge issued his verdict only a few hours before the planned transmission time of the film. In a ruling which was to become famous, he ordered the channel, 'bearing in mind the nature of the countless scenes of sexual perversion which the film *Joy et Joan* contains, not to show the film before 10.30 pm or else it would have to pay a fine of one million francs.'

This ruling naturally set a precedent in case law for its exemplary character. On the one hand, it laid down, in principle, that a soft porn film that was forbidden to the under-sixteens could harm the sensitivity of child and teenage viewers by being shown on television during peak time. Furthermore, the 10.30 pm slot was virtually made official as the 'Watershed'. Finally, and this is perhaps the most important aspect, the judge reminded people that, although the law could impose a particular transmission time for such broadcasts, it could not ban or censor them.

Table 5. Directive of 5 May 1989 concerning the protection of children and adolescents in the programming of broadcasts transmitted by public and private television services

The amended law of 30 September 1986 entrusts the Conseil superieur de l'audiovisuel with the task of watching over the protection of children and adolescents in the programming of broadcasts transmitted by audiovisual communication services.

Concerned about the scheduling and transmission of broadcasts likely to affect this objective, the Conseil calls upon those responsible for editorial matters in public and private broadcasting, and asks them strictly to adhere to a principle solemnly affirmed by parliament.

To this effect, the Conseil superieur de l'audiovisuel considers it necessary to formulate measures, to be adopted by public and private television services to help achieve the objective, and which will guide the Conseil's actions.

1. The Company must ensure that it does not broadcast transmissions for young people involving scenes likely to offend the sensitivity of those for whom the programmes are intended.

2. The company must ensure that programmes during peak broadcast times are intended for a family audience.

3. The company shall refrain from broadcasting programmes, in particular cinematic or video works, of an erotic nature or those likely to incite to violence, between 6.00am and 10.30pm. It must in particular ensure that advertisements for these broadcasts are not shown before 8.30pm and that they do not contain scenes likely to offend the sensitivity of children and adolescents.

4. The company must warn television viewers, in an appropriate manner, when it is scheduling and broadcasting programmes likely to offend their sensitivity, and particularly audiences made up of children and adolescents. This warning must accompany any presentation made on air of the broadcast concerned.

5. No film contrary to accepted standards shall be broadcast by the company.

Jacques Boutet
Chairman
Conseil superieur de l'audiovisuel
Paris
5 May 1989

When a new law on audiovisual matters was brought in at the start of 1989, the Counseil Supérieur de l'Audiovisuel (CSA) succeeded the CNCL as the regulator of

French broadcasting. The CSA set about working out a plan for a 'directive on the protection of childhood and adolescence' which was aimed at broadcasters (see Table 5).

A letter sent to all broadcasters in June 1989 laid down the stipulation that the film classification categories of the Commission de Classification des Films Cinémato-graphiques be transferred to films on television.

Thus broadcasters were advised not to show films, forbidden to the under-twelves, before 10.00 pm, and not to show films forbidden to the under-sixteens before 10.30 pm. The showing of X-rated films and cinema films banned to the under-eighteens is only permitted on an encrypted service which has additional access limitations (PIN-code or card) and there are very precise scheduling restrictions (midnight to five o'clock in the morning.[15]

In the case of programmes other than cinematographic material, that is, programmes which are not the subject of a prior classification (TV fiction, magazine programmes, etc.), the CSA has recommended that internal viewing committees be set up within the channels, which are given the task of deciding upon an appropriate transmission time for programmes that might not be suitable for children and teenagers.

The steps taken by the CSA, following the adoption of the directive, were fairly numerous and dynamic. They could be accompanied by penalty proceedings culmi-nating in quite heavy fines. However, in virtually all cases, the procedures related to the presentation and depiction of violence rather than sex.

In the last ten years, French television has undergone considerable legal, financial and social transformations. The abandonment of the state service monopoly, some de-regulation, the laws on competition, the development of true-to-life TV are just some of the factors which have altered the face of programming. The taboos which had surrounded the depiction of sex on television for a long time have been lifted on the grounds of freedom of communication; on financial grounds, as the race to capture an audience gathers; on more sociological grounds, as society and mores evolves. There has been no doubt some abuse of this transformation and this, in itself, has justified the measures taken by the regulator who, on questions concerning eroticism and pornography on the screen, finds he must tread a fine line between the rights of the freedom to communicate versus the protection of children and teenagers.

---

15 In the opinion of the CSA, the showing of pornographic films moreover contravenes the terms of Article 22 of the European directive on 'television without frontiers'. However, EEC rules on this point have not been transposed into French law.

Laughing at other people's private parts

by Armando Iannucci

Victoria Wood has a short routine about a couple who have sexual intercourse on a train while there are other passengers present in the carriage. None of the other passengers say a word, and resolutely stick to reading their newspapers or looking out the window. Eventually, the couple stop what they are doing, get off the floor and light up some post coital cigarettes, at which point an old lady opposite leans over and says 'Excuse me, Do you mind? This is a No Smoking Carriage'.

I suppose this joke strikes home because it highlights an extremely prevalent and stubborn British attitude towards sex, which is to pretend that it does not happen. (Indeed, an incident rather similar to the one above was reported in the press as actually having occurred earlier this year.)

Those who are shocked by the depiction of sexual activity on our television screens are possibly affected not so much by the explicit nature of the representation as by the extent to which it acts as an unavoidable reminder of something they would rather not think about. The shock is compounded when there are others present in the room, for the troubled viewer then knows that what he or she would prefer to keep secret has in fact been made public knowledge. If the others in the room are one's own children, then the whole affair becomes ten times as embarrassing: a combination of stifled smirks and innocent disapproval greet the eye from the little one's faces as they realize for the first time just what kind of a sordid activity you have been up to.

It is a mark of just how embarrassed we are by the sex act that we reserve discussion of it mostly for humorous or jokey conversation. Until very recently, British humour has been distinguished by its near total obsession with sauciness. Our country's greatest contribution to the cinema has been the *Carry On* movie (that, and *James Bond*, whose attitude towards sex is equally dubious) and we have made an art-form out of the double entendre, a complex linguistic labyrinth where dirty ideas are driven underground and lurk beneath the surface of substitute words.

Nowadays, we like to think we are a little bit more grown up about these things. A new wave of comedians claim to have radicalized the joke-agenda by relieving us of our clumsy notions of sexual stereotypes and up-rooting a few taboos, but in practice all this means is that our screens are now filled with 'knob' jokes rather than breast gags, and that it is OK to use the word 'clitoris' in a punchline. As a comedy producer who likes to pretend he works at the cutting edge of dangerous comedy, it is frequently dispiriting to see how often the biggest laugh still comes from a nice bit of innuendo. It is funny, though.

Our apparent and newly acquired maturity on these matters has produced a rather interesting phenomenon, the rehabilitation of pornography. That new breed of male, the New Lad, while taking pains to demonstrate his care and empathy for the female and all her dilemmas, now feels liberated enough to celebrate his own needs and desires in the company of other men; uninhibited talk in the locker-room about football, about cars, drink and sexual conquests are regarded as fit subjects for discourse. In this re-assertion of maleness, pornography has for the first time been casually and openly acknowledged as an accepted source of enjoyment and stimulation. Similarly, any survey of the current stand-up comedy circuit will readily uncover a willingness to talk in detail about pornography, masturbation and the like as matter-of-fact events in the lives of the (male) comic's audience.

The New Woman has rejoindered by adjusting the traditional anti-pornographic stance of the feminist, who rested her original argument on pornography's blatant forms of exploitation by men of women, and she now argues for an equivalent access to a pornography marketed at her sex too. The recent launch of *For Women* magazine, with its artfully shot male full-frontal wrapped in cellophane, *Company* magazine's recent and notorious pull-out on The Penis, and the celebrity status accredited to a bunch of strippers called *The Chippendales* are examples of this acceptance of the public availability of titillation as a valid form of entertainment.

Now, of course, all this begs the question; are the above examples 'pornographic'? There is a strong case here for arguing for a redefinition of the word. Neither the New Man nor the New Woman would seek the actual exploitation of members of the opposite sex in this form for entertainment; it is all good clean fun, with the full and happy consent of all those being covered in clingfilm or waving their bits at a polaroid. The only point being made is that sex is enjoyable and unavoidable, and ought to be regarded without embarrassment.

It is interesting how rapidly this point of view is being fed into mainstream opinion. Video copies of *The Lover's Guide* now sit happily on domestic mantelpieces, alongside *Ghost* and *ET*, while Programme Controllers at the BBC are quite happy to schedule heaving buttocks quiveringly close to the Watershed. Sex on the radio, always an elliptical affair, has exploded in the form of unexpurgated readings from *Lady Chatterly's Lover* and *Ulysses* as well as fairly frank anatomical discussions on Radio Four at ten-thirty in the morning on *Woman's Hour*. The need to address the AIDS questions head on with a previously uncommon frankness has had a knock-on effect throughout the schedules. A vivid illustration is the BBC's recently invested kudos and, more importantly, ten million pounds, in the unashamedly Club 18–30 mix of sun, sand and sex at 7.00 pm with the flaccid *Eldorado*, the moral agenda for which was firmly set in the opening episode's classic line, 'I tell you what. I wouldn't mind giving her one'. Youth culture too has seemed more at ease with the subject and on

Radio One, often in the past prone to quite arbitrary attacks of prudery, it is common-place to hear at eight in the morning The breakfast Crew introduce the likes of *Everybody's Having Sex, I'm Too Sexy, Love Sex Intelligence, Let's Talk About Sex* with a frequency at that time of the morning which is more than a little alarming.

The effect of all this is, I think, to split the populace into two fuzzy groups. On the one hand there are those relics of a not too distant age who would have preferred not to see or hear such things other than in coy conversation or harmless seaside innuendo, who are not frightened by sex but who feel the activity is a private matter not up for public scrutiny or mockery. Staring and laughing at them in the face is the second camp, who have no desire to run rampant but who are much more at home with a reasonably inhibited expression of sexuality. Most people probably lie somewhere in between the two but with, I think, a definite inclination to one or other point of view.

The problems start when we have to appoint arbiters of public taste on these matters. Trying to define how far you can go, it seems, has become a matter of less and less objective determination. It is a simple solution to establish a series of time zones throughout the schedules which mark the degree of sexual frankness which can be depicted on our screens and through our radios; only the casual unbuttoning of a tie in early evening, toe sucking by eight pm, carefully filmed partial nudity around nine, all-out graphic sex scenes in the wee small hours, and so on. But this is to concentrate the debate purely on what can be shown, and not on what can be discussed. Very few would sensibly argue for graphic sex scenes at any time of day on any of the main national networks, but an increasing number of people would argue for a much more liberated attitude towards what can be *mentioned*. There is now at last one, and perhaps several, generations for whom contraception, sex outside marriage, homo-sexuality, single parenthood, etc. are accepted facets and norms of daily life causing little or no controversy when raised in matter-of-fact conversation. But what happens when our country's moral guardians are neither part of that generation nor adopt the same pervasive attitude to sexual matters? How easily can someone who firmly believes there is a time and a place to discuss sex understand and empathize with someone who holds that sex, like shopping, music, or food, is a matter to be discussed or ignored whatever the mood suits?

I ask these questions as someone who has been accused, tried, found guilty and flogged by the Broadcasting Standards Council on this matter. *Loose Talk*, a production of mine for Radio One, takes stand-up comics from the circuit, puts them in front of a typical audience of Radio One listeners, and answers their questions on the week's news in an entertaining and, hopefully amusing way. We recorded a programme from Brighton the week the Archbishop of Canterbury was due to meet the Pope and shortly after he had just declared his bewilderment at the Roman Catholic Church's stance on contraception. It was also about the time the Bishop of Galway admitted to fathering a child in America. It was fairly inevitable, really, that a question concerning the Church's attitude to sex was in the offing, and I considered a heady brew of sex and religion very much suited to the programmes's fairly direct style.

I did, but someone else did not, and that person, without giving away the BSC's confidentiality, was a senior clergyman of the Church of England.* Why was he listening to Radio One on a Saturday night when he should have been working on his Sunday morning sermon I do not know. However, when the conversation got round to God's approval of sex, and, indeed, God's experience and enjoyment of sex, one listener got a little hot under the dog-collar. More or less the next thing I knew was that the matter was up before the Council and that the clergyman's objection had been upheld.

I suppose this is neither the time nor the place to question the Council's judgement, but since at the time the BBC were in no hurry to ask for my account I don't have many qualms in exploiting this opportunity here. The whole problem rests on one of attitude to sexual activity. Either you think that sex is an unspoken thing, a secret, slightly furtive, hidden activity, with perhaps more than a little lust or moral failing associated with it, or you do not. If you think the former then, of course, to link sex with the Deity is a shocking collocation to make. However, if your position is that there is nothing, absolutely nothing, wrong with sex as an activity, then it becomes a pretty clear demonstration of your faith in this opinion to mention it in connection with God without a single qualm. Both attitudes are subjective, though conflicting, stances arising from two very different mind-sets, and both, of course, must be respected. The question is, how do you judge which mind-set is *objectively* more worthy of respect.

One method would be to establish the prevailing mind-set of the listenership or viewership at any given moment. Since the remarks in question were recorded in front of a typical cross-section of the Radio One audience, who all, judging by their laughter and applause, approved the remarks, and given that the programme received very, very few complaints from listeners at home, it would appear that, in general, the comic's expressed views about sex were shared by the overwhelming majority of those listening to him.

Why then does the Council uphold a subjective opinion held by a demonstrably *atypical* listener? Is it because it judges all such remarks against an objective Code of Practice, consisting of lists of quantified degrees of permitted shock set against specific hours of the day, across all networks? Or is it because the prevailing mind-set within it does not match the set of attitudes listening to the broadcast in question, and so, quite understandably, cannot come to terms with them?

Either way, it seems that some modifications in the Council's Code may be useful. It may be necessary to adjust our present reliance on the Watershed system to take into account different types of audience on different networks. What may cause offence to a Radio Four listener at any hour of the day may seem perfectly harmless to a Radio One listener, and guidelines for one network should never be applied to another. Similarly, it may be that the Council could benefit from widening its own panel of opinion-makers to take into account shifting attitudes towards social, moral and ethical issues within the generations. They have my name and address.

When publishing the Bulletin containing its Findings, the Council usually gives the name and county of the first complainant.

Memorandum: Sex on TV

by Patrick Stoddart

To: Head of Plays

From: Director of Programme Exploitation

Dear HoP

You are going to love this one. I have an idea for an action series in which one of the central characters is a good-looking woman, forever being trapped in sexually compromising situations. We could dress her up in extremely tight-fitting leather, and it would really help the male 25–40 demographics if, on most weeks, she was lashed to a bed/rafter/threshing machine/railway line/household appliance, and then threatened by a succession of leering men. Do I have a go on this one?

Frankly, I suspect that poor Head of DoPE would not get his go. It is hard to imagine the Director General of the BBC, the ITV central scheduler or even the Channel 4 Commissioning Editor for Really Shocking Bits going dizzy with enthusiasm at the idea of a popular drama serial in which bondage, rape fantasies and sexual innuendo were regular weekly fixtures. Yet in 1962, exactly 30 years ago, not a hair was turned when Honor Blackman first slipped into something uncomfortable for *The Avengers*.

It could be that most of us were simply too innocent to understand the sexual significance of all that straining leather, and for all I know the people who made *The Avengers* were no wiser than the rest of us. But I doubt that – it is hard to believe that such sophisticated TV folk were not having a little fun at the expense of the naivety of viewers in Bolton, Basildon and the Brompton Road.

The Avengers was not the only programme to flaunt sex, just – in hindsight – the most obvious. What is interesting, however, is that television in the upfront nineties could never get away with anything remotely like it, because the medium itself has been almost too successful in educating its audience.

Television, through everything from Bernard Manning and Bond movies to dramas ponderous with social realism, has done a great deal to rid us of the curse of innocence – indeed, it has broadened our carnal knowledge to the extent that most of us are now smart enough to spot a sexual encounter three scenes before it happens, and the result of that new wisdom is that television has now effectively shackled itself against any attempts to experiment too often with the way it handles the subject.

At the same time, it has also informed – perhaps even invented – the new and largely admirable science of political correctness, which means that the nudgery of the 1960s and 1970s, which if nothing else had the educative benefits of the bike shed, has now been banned from the screen, leaving producers with two commandments to choose from. The first, from the Greer Academy, is 'Do it properly', the second, from the Whitehouse Church, is 'Don't do it at all', and nothing much survives in between.

There is rich irony in this polarization of moral rectitude. On one hand, sex on television is not as hard to find as it once was (there is no hiding place for the simple and sweaty heavings of *The Men's Room*), while on the other hand, it can certainly be found less often – partly because television mirrors life itself, with every outburst of frenzied sexual activity being followed by a long period of rest, as producers find a haven from the storm that must be ridden out before it is safe to embark on another voyage of sexual discovery.

Despite the worst forebodings of the lobby for creative liberty, such storm warnings do not, on the whole, emanate from the Broadcasting Standards Council, which defines only the most obvious excesses as clearly unacceptable, and otherwise leaves it to programme makers to use their common sense. It is only when common sense evaporates that the BSC pounces, and it does not pounce very often. According to its latest Annual Report, the BSC received a total of 349 complaints on matters dealing with sex, violence and sex, or taste and decency and sex in the year ending May 1992, and it rejected all but 12 of them.

It is not the regulators, but the unregulated, unfettered popular press that swoops at the slightest sign of movement, and their role in the sexual development of broadcasting is much harder to define or defend. The tabloids are past masters at boiling complicated issues down to their bones (or perhaps to their flesh) which usually means that television's restless quest to find the right balance in its portrayal of sexual activity is translated into: 'Is there too much bonking on the box?' And the tabloids, whose circulation figures rely heavily on people bonking as often and indiscreetly as possible, invariably conclude that there is, and a terrible thing it is too.

The double-vision and instant whip opinions of the tabloids should not matter, but they do. Try, as they may, programme makers cannot totally trust their own instincts when they know that a handful of rags will be thrust in their faces, claiming to represent the tastes of 20 million viewers – even if the tabloids are actually more interested in dictating the agenda, rather than following it.

The heat generated by all that paper-fuelled passion often scorches the wrong targets, given that many regular tabloid readers regard such ranting hypocrisy with more amusement than amazement, and that most of them are perfectly able to cope with the sporadic sight of naked bodies without recourse to counselling, the courts, or a call to the duty officer. But the tabloids are in the noise business. When they scream, MPs listen, and for want of anything better to do, they ask questions in the House – if only for an excuse to grind an axe about the licence fee or the continuing power of the pink conspiracy.

Often, this will be the first thing a significant slice of viewers hear about the matter anyway, because for a variety of reasons, they neither know nor care about the sexual state of play on television. There is precious little of it in *Neighbours, Coronation Street* or *Wheel of Fortune*, and by the time anything remotely questionable reaches the screen, a growing number of them will in any case have turned off the terrestrial channels to watch a saga of rape and disembowelment on video or satellite.

This brings us to a peculiar truth. While the debate over sex on television usually centres on what damage might be done to the vulnerable working masses, the fact is that sex very rarely occurs in the kind of programme that section of society prefers to watch.

Indeed, a large proportion of the sex scenes which have caused so much angst in recent years has been contained in television's more articulate drama output – *The Camomile Lawn, Oranges Are Not The Only Fruit, Blackeyes, The Singing Detective* etc. – most of which have been aimed at what is perceived as the selective minority who watch BBC2 and Channel 4. If anything, television sex is a delicacy made for and by a particular middle class group, and it is handled not with the tacky enthusiasm of the tabloid press, but the meticulous prurience of *The Daily Telegraph*. It could be argued, of course, that this is one way of keeping a difficult matter in safe hands, but it also suggests that broadcasters do not consider the great viewing masses to be fit persons for the consumption of adult drama.

This is not a covert appeal for total licence, only for a more realistic and consistent approach, unencumbered by the sectional interests of politicians, press and pressure groups, which would dull the edge of outrage and allow broadcasters to find a more coherent context for sex on television. And until sex itself is accepted as a natural part of the broadcasting diet (even if, like fatty food, it should be taken in moderation), programme makers will continue to be discouraged from tackling what a police officer might call 'matters pertaining thereto'.

One example. Violence in sex is a grim fact of late 20th century life, and it has very properly been the subject of innumerable documentaries. But as with homelessness, drug abuse and a depressing variety of other urgent social issues, it is only when popular drama intervenes that the matter breaks out of the ghetto of concerned thought and on to a broader public agenda. Yet rape remains an unexploded bomb for all who attempt to deal with it.

For perfectly sound reasons, the current orthodoxy is that it is irresponsible and provocative to show the act itself, any pleasure in the face of the man committing it, or indeed the anguish on the face of the woman suffering it. But averting the gaze merely fudges the issue, denies the truth and leaves nothing in the mind but an uneasy sense of voyeurism – an unsatisfactory combination that persuades most pragmatic directors and producers to avoid the subject altogether. In recent memory, the only popular drama series to portray rape and its consequences with anything approaching candour has been *EastEnders*, and the BBC did not escape that brave decision without being accused of exploitation, sensationalism and the corruption of young viewers.

The corruption of young women, however, seems to have become a staple part of

113

drama recently. In both *A Sense of Guilt* and *A Time to Dance*, two of the most avidly debated serials of the past year, the plot concerned men in mid-life seducing (or being seduced by) girls young enough to be their daughters. It seems strange that the sexual fantasies of men in mid-life crisis are considered suitable material for drama, when rape – which many psychologists would say lies behind that fantasy – is not.

It is, of course, equally important to talk about sex as it is to demonstrate it, and there is a pressing need to break such discussions out of the smug womb of late night Channel 4 talk shows, which at worst only titillate, and at best do no more to put the matter on an open agenda than the Pope and Victoria Gillick debating the pros and cons of contraception.

This is never going to be as easy as it sounds, as I know from personal experience. Some years ago, I wrote and presented a series for ITV called *The Video Age*, which attempted to do for the rental trade what Barry Norman does for the cinema. We were also keen to attack what were then the twin monsters of video nasties and video porn, but as the show went out at 12.30 pm – immediately after *Rainbow* and before the lunchtime news – it proved impossible to show anything other than me, looking like a recently-goosed vicar, muttering things along the lines of: 'If you'd seen what I've seen, you'd be outraged'. If it achieved anything at all, the programme probably made viewers more curious to see for themselves, rather than to warn them that there was material out there that would have shocked a satanist serial killer.

Our problems were partly caused by the time slot, but the ever-closing jaws of political correctness and moral sensibility would still make life difficult, at any point in the schedule, to this day. Before any future outbreaks of unpleasantness can be tackled responsibly, the verbal, as well as the visual, language of sex must find its way back on to popular television.

And there are signs of that happening. While there should be no return to 'take my wife' jokes and *Benny Hill* sketches, the rules of honest reflection still apply, and indeed are now being applied in another, newer, BBC soap opera – it is no coincidence that the clip used in early trailers for *Eldorado* showed a perfectly-made Spanish girl bouncing up and down on a horse without the aid of a safety harness.

It is not easy to make a sturdy defence of a soap opera which bases its appeal on the lascivious yearnings of a group of tax dodgers, crooks and medallion men, but it is at least accurate in their portrayal. Nobody would argue that a sizable percentage of those who choose to live in the hacienda-style urbanizations of southern Spain are lured there by the promise of sex in the sun, and that much of their day is spent trying to find it.

At the time of writing, we have not yet seen the act performed, and at the time of transmission, I doubt we ever will, but they do talk about it a lot. And if most of the male characters in *Eldorado* discuss most of its female characters in the language of Essex Man, it does have a ring of truth. By stripping away the pretensions and getting the dialogue down to the level of 'I wouldn't mind giving that Consuela a good seeing to', *Eldorado* is at least describing characters that its target audience can recognize, while the toilet free zone of *Neighbours* merely lies about a world in which Pollyanna would think that every day was her birthday.

114

It remains to be seen whether the dirtier denizens of *Eldorado* can teach younger viewers anything other than the wrong way to talk to women, but on the evidence of *EastEnders*, *Brookside* and the rest, it must be assumed that the producers have a grander plan for them somewhere down the road. And if the device of sex talk holds the audience's attention long enough for them to become interested in the more serious facts of life, then *Eldorado* might yet prove that the unlovely language of the Dagenham wine bar has its uses.

Sex and sexuality

by Sally Munt

L ike other ten-year olds, I used to surreptitiously switch on the old black and white television in my bedroom well after my Mother thought I'd gone to sleep over my *Jackie* magazine. One night, bored with Cathy and Claire's advice to slim down, slap up, and stand around waiting for That Man via one kiss to transport me to an unspecified and vague rapture (this is a pre-adolescent sexual fantasy remember), my eyes slid to the silent television whereupon I saw something I *knew* I should not. Soundlessly (Mum could hear up four flights), two women were kissing. One of them was dressed as a man. It was rude. It was exciting. It did not turn me into a lesbian.[16]

Twenty-two years later I recall the thrill of witnessing that quintessentially 1970 moment. I learned it was a scene from Ken Russell's made-for-television biography of Richard Strauss, *Dance of the Seven Veils* which caused a huge controversy concerning the limits of broadcasting decency. 1970 was also at the hub of emerging sexual liberation movements: hip people were grooving, swinging, and letting it all hang (dropping) out. Sexual expression, distilled into the act of sex itself, was seen as facilitating the liberation of an identity, a personal core that was deeply truthful, integral and honest. Sexual intimacy, according to this belief, was the celebration of an authentic selfhood. Sexual freedom was to be a healing force, not just for the repressed individual, but for society itself.

The idea that sexuality should come out of the bedroom and be understood as political was primarily perceived as being a counter-cultural perspective. The Gay Liberation Front was forming even as I confronted my first queer kiss, at that den of perversion, the London School of Economics, in Autumn 1970. By privileging Gay Pride the early GLF was prepared to challenge the myth of sexuality as somehow separate and protected from the influence of the social world. Gay Gloom was a product of prejudice, not predestiny. Coming out as gay or lesbian was about rejecting the predominant construction of homosexuality as sinful, sick, and over-sexed. Contemporary media stereotypes had colluded with this view in films such as *The Killing of Sister George* (1968), which was overlaid with a sado-masochistic desperation.

---

16 I am grateful to Keith Howse for this information.

Politicized sexual identities promoting a positive image of homosexuality make many heterosexuals uncomfortable. Contained within the idea that gay and lesbian people can remake their identity as something attractive and desirable is an implicit mutability inferring that (a) sexuality is not a pre-(God) given state of nature, (b) sexuality is produced by social forces, and that therefore c) different forms of sexuality can be promoted or discouraged according to certain political agendas. This is a very scary thought. Attempts to control media representations of homosexuality by 'pro-family' Right-wing pressure groups are informed by this idea, for theirs is the fear that homosexuality is contagious, since it is a 'disease', it can be catching. The conflation of homosexuality with AIDS in the public imagination resulting in the moral panic over the 'Gay Plague' (for which the media must take some responsibility), clinches the connection.

But, if homosexuals can be made, then the obverse must be true: heterosexuals can be made too. Heterosexuality mutates under variable historical and cultural conditions. What heterosexuals were doing in and out of the bedroom in 1892 is not the same as what they are doing now. Similarly, what heterosexuals are doing in Manchuria is not the same as what they are doing in Manchester, or Muine Bheag, Southern Ireland. Anal penetration by the penis is taboo in some cultures, but a necessary form of contraception, and a form of pleasure in others. Active female sexuality is encouraged in some cultures, and viciously punished in others. Sometimes both behaviours are expected in the same culture, but with two different women, in the old chestnut the virgin/whore opposition.

Sex is a bit of a performance, isn't it. The discrete categories of heterosexuality and homosexuality are perhaps better understood as myths of social organization (I am not proposing a universal model of human bisexuality here either, which simply collapses the former duality into a new imposed category). To paraphrase Freud: perversity is diversity, and we cannot speculate on what human sexuality might be like loosed from the constraints of civilization, because we cannot step outside to know. But what we can do, and do do (Freudians make of that slip what you like), is to extrapolate the boundaries of our experience to shift, combine, push against, and reconstruct our sexual identity according to what we see around us. Sometimes that involves retrenchment, sometimes, it means making ourselves anew.

Inevitably popular representations have a powerful influence on this process, and the history of television is saturated with fears that viewers passively emulate everything they see. Paranoia about television's effects becomes epidemical when adults discuss children. Youth is constructed as a state of innocence infinitely corruptible by popular culture – before television there were comics, or gangster films, more recently 'video nasties' have been carrying the can. The child is a metaphor for the family under threat from external enemies. The family unit is thus a state of harmonized nature being attacked by a demonized culture. The adults' responsibility is as gatekeepers, protecting the child from the taint of unacceptable outside influences. Sexual knowledge, as for Adam and Eve, precipitates the Fall.

But the family, however loving, also contains it own violence. Taking the issue of widespread child sexual abuse from *within* the family aside for one moment, how many of us grew up with nearest and dearests resembling *The Cosby Show*? Jealousy,

117

cruelty, neglect and rejection are part of the experience of family life, and any healthy child expresses her or his violent feelings as a visible response to this. Similarly, children do not suddenly become sexual at the age of consent (sixteen for heterosexuals, twenty-one for male homosexuals). Childhood sexuality is already a complex negotiation for them of the permissible and the forbidden. Early erotic attachments undoubtably do affect later sexual identities, but this process is an unstable, unpredictable one.

The central problem contained within a piece of published research such as this is the attempt to grapple with effects theory viz if I see two women kissing for a few seconds on television at an impressionable age, will this turn me into a lesbian? Well, I read *Jackie* magazine from cover-to-cover for the five years framing this fleeting image, but this failed to turn me into a heterosexual (permanently anyhow). Does this then prove the potency of the perverse image? Can one brief glance at a queer sex scene countermand hundreds of hours of heterosexuality? I am parodying the latent anxiety in effects theory in order to draw attention to the often ludicrous transference of power granted to the Other, usually a subcultural (and by implication subversive) group, to transform dominant society.

Despite the determined efforts of sexologists from the late nineteenth century to the present to locate the origin of homosexuality in either nature or nurture, we are still no clearer in establishing whether gays and lesbians are ultimately born 'that way', or made. Along a continuum, however, we can say that identity is formed in relation to external (social) and internal (psychic) constraints. An immeasurable range of them. This is why effects theory is notoriously unreliable. Studies abound on the relationship between pornography and sexual behaviour, and cases can be made for both liberalization and censorship, depending on who interprets the data. Human subjects being studied in laboratory conditions do not behave in the same way at home. Similarly, the variables present in a social setting precludes any empirical evidence being established, except of a limited applicability. Hence many judgements made by effects theorists have often been self-fulfilling and commonsensical.

One example of this from early television analysis is the hypodermic model. Briefly, this idea states that viewers consist of an inert, alienated and undifferentiated mass susceptible to the hypnotic indoctrination of destructive desires which can only lead to delinquency or brain death. Television watching is a one-way-street. Cultural Studies research since the 1970s has consistently contested this view, pointing out the implied patronage of this model – that it consisted of middle-class intellectuals 'studying' the working-classes, assuming their subjects lumpenly conformed to their preconceived notions. A more recent, but similarly condescending, version of this materializes on the Left with the 'politically correct' viewing being decided by elite cultural theorists who then tell ordinary punters whether they are allowed to find pleasure in the narrative, or whether they should boycott the product on principle for being 'right off'. Rather, people watch television in a variety of active and self-conscious ways, negotiating sophisticated codes, interpreting according to a range of criteria including their own social identity, and often refusing the preferred meaning in a text and supplanting it with their own.

Allowing then, for this view that television has a significant, but *contingent* effect upon consumers and that people often read televisual messages perversely, are we still left with a guileless gutless group of gudgeons who will gullibly swallow the bait of a gay kiss and rush out to reproduce it? Maybe the infamous (no tongues) kiss between Colin and Guido on *EastEnders* in 1989 did put ideas in some people's heads, but could this image, or the handful of similar representations of gay and lesbian sexuality on television really convert men and women from a life of consummate heterosexuality?

The intention of this essay is to stimulate some discussion concerning why so many people find the representation of gay or lesbian sexuality on television so offensive. Precisely because homosexuality has been discursively linked with the hypersexual these representations are doubly marked as sexual, and hence, by some, obscene. That homosexuals are always 'at it' is a cliche not just of pornography but of mainstream media conventions too. Homosexuality becomes the marker of the boundary between the illicit and the permissible of screen sexuality. Within this zone there is a diversity of forms for the visual representation of homosexuality, which I identify as follows:

(i) *Tragicomic stereotypes:* of the John Inman variety. Plus there is a whole history of unhappy homosexuals I haven't the space to inventorize here.

(ii) *Problem television:* of which there are there main derivatives, firstly the chat show which concentrates on the 'My son is gay, what shall I do?' dilemma; secondly the moral/religious programme dealing with the ethics of the gay replication of 'hetero-sexual' family structures such as marriage or adoption (these programmes have a mainly liberal, integrationist undercurrent); thirdly the plethora of programmes on AIDS, from dramatic reconstructions to late-night discussion programmes. These broadcasts are directed at a heterosexual viewer.

(iii) *Anthropological/lifestyle series:* referring here largely to Channel 4's magazine programme *Out on Tuesday*, now *Out*, produced by a variety of lesbian and gay programme makers and intended for a lesbian or gay viewer under the channel's remit for minority audiences and experimental television. London Weekend Television produced a precursor series *Gay Life* in 1981 and 1982 which crossed over between these two categories, but because of its indeterminate identity as being neither specifically *for* or *about* gays, it died. Nevertheless, as a pilot it can now be seen as a pioneering first. *Out* recruits about a million viewers, and has been successful in affirming existing lesbian and gay identities, and it has also appealed to the 'sympath-etic straight' viewer in 'explaining' homosexuality in terms more of its own making (cf. similarities to (ii) above). Its lifestyle magazine format has utilized an anthropo-logical viewpoint which serves a crucial function of reflecting a subculture back onto itself, enhancing a group identity and the sense of a community of viewers. Histori-cally the series has been constrained into a 'positive images' approach, mindful of the homophobic majority of media stereotypes it needs to counterbalance, and the spectre of the ubiquitous homophobic spectator. Now more established, the series can afford more controversy, as the recent piece on gay skinheads demonstrated. The most radical aspect of *Out* is its ability to portray same-sex *relationships,* i.e. not that men or women can have sex with each other, but that they can love each other, and even be happy. This is perceived as a threat to the perception of the nuclear family as being the universally true, only normal, natural and 'right' model of human organization.

(iv) *Art cinema:* Because of the historical conflation between art, the avant garde and

119

homosexuality (embodied in the narcissistic aesthete Dorian Gray), and because high culture has a privileged status of utterance in Western society – and also because some of our most prestigious producers of art have been unavoidably and unequivocally homosexual – art cinema is allowed a 'contained' articulation of homosexual desire. Maintaining the 'integrity of the text' (not a common defence employed by popular culture) has meant that television – primarily Channel 4 but also BBC2 – has been allowed to transmit uncut films containing explicit and formally innovative representations which would not be permissible in popular genres. Derek Jarman's films illustrate this loophole. Because the implied reader is a discerning intellectual, s/he is less likely to indulge in copycat behaviour. The liberal arts establishment has defended freedom of expression under the aegis of excellence, an allocation of value which has become increasingly contested.

(v) *Romance fiction:* a more naturalistic form which nevertheless distances representations of homosexuality by deploying the veil of history. Set in the past (*Brideshead Revisited, Oranges are Not the Only Fruit, Portrait of a Marriage*), the evocation of a period defuses the threat. (It also means the subject of AIDS can be avoided.) Costume drama, with its strong fantasy conventions, reinforces this strangeness. Recourse to the original literary text as justification can legitimate some very challenging images however – the cry 'it's in the novel' lending credence to the view that if it's art, it's in (the lesbian rape scene in *Portrait of a Marriage* was one of the most radical scenes on television). Romance fiction provides the most subversive form in which homosexuality is reproduced on television because of the processes of identification inscribed within the romance narrative. Precisely because it provides such an emotional hook, because the spectator engages so directly with the trajectory of the protagonist, the distancing frame of heterosexuality/homosexuality, with the latter marked so clearly as Other, breaks down.

Does the heterosexual spectator temporarily occupy a homosexual viewing position when she/he becomes 'lost' in the captivating moment of a lesbian/gay romance? Perhaps. Fleetingly. It is this process of identification which is so threatening to the homophobic viewer. But this brief moment, however heartfelt, will not destroy the institution of heterosexuality sustaining the foundations of Western Society. It creates a moment of empathy, an *imaginative* sharing of experience which is in the realm of fantasy. Television is a powerful medium which is sometimes subtly coercive, but it is not a simple propaganda instrument. Viewers are complex social subjects negotiating a plethora of persuasive and often contradictory influences. The construction of certain meanings cannot be assumed, and concomitant effects upon personal behaviour are notoriously difficult to establish, despite attempts by discrete interest groups to 'prove' a causal connection. Given the current level of signposting employed by broadcasters to contextualize and contain images of sexuality, audiences are well able to make up their own minds, without censorship.

I am indebted to Andy Medhurst for talking through the ideas above, and for his particular insights. In addition I would like to thank Caroline Spry of Channel 4 and Mandy Merck of Fulcrum Productions, for agreeing to be interviewed and for their helpful direction.

Appendix 1: The variables

Variables influencing comment on proportion of violence, sex and bad language on television

The following tables show those variables which were found to be key in attitudes expressed about the proportion of violence, sex and bad language on television.

Table A shows that, for each topic considered, age and gender were prime variables affecting opinion. So that, the older the respondent, the more likely she/he was to consider that there was too much violence, sex or bad language on television. In addition, female respondents were more likely to say this than male respondents.

Parents broadly were as concerned as the sample at large by the amount of violence, sex and bad language shown on television. What is particularly worth noting is the finding that parents' concerns generally increased as their children grew older (Table B). Parents with children in their early teens (and slightly younger) and those parents with adult children still living at home were significantly more concerned about the amount of violence, sex and bad language on television.

In all cases, another important variable in attitudes to the depiction of the above events on television was the practice of a religion – respondents who regularly attended religious services were more likely to say that there was too much violence, sex and bad language on television than the sample as a whole.

Table A. Effect of variables of age and gender

	Too much %	About right %	Too little %
Violence			
Total	66	32	2
M 13–17*	29	54	16
M 18–34	40	53	6
M 35–54	57	40	3
M 55+	76	24	1
F 13–17*	47	50	3
F 18–34	75	25	–
F 35–54	76	23	1
F 55+	85	14	–
Sex			
Total	41	54	4
M 13–17*	14	79	7
M 18–34	16	71	12
M 35–54	26	67	7
M 55+	60	39	1
F 13–17*	28	69	3
F 18–34	30	64	5
F 35–54	41	58	1
F 55+	82	18	–
Bad language			
Total	60	38	2
M 13–17*	46	49	4
M 18–34	39	53	6
M 35–54	58	39	3
M 55+	67	33	–
F 13–17*	48	48	5
F 18–34	56	44	–
F 35–54	67	33	–
F 55+	80	19	–

*Small sample sizes
Base: 1137 respondents, all expressing opinion.

Table B. Variables affecting parents' comments about television

	Too much %	About right %	Too little %
Violence			
All parents	69	29	1
With children:			
aged 0–7	66	33	1
aged 8–10	71	27	2
aged 11–12	78	20	1
aged 13–17	73	26	1
aged 18+	72	26	2
Sex			
All parents	36	59	4
With children:			
aged 0–7	29	66	6
aged 8–10	28	65	6
aged 11–12	37	60	2
aged 13–17	35	59	5
aged 18+	55	45	–
Bad language			
All parents	62	36	1
With children:			
aged 0–7	57	41	2
aged 8–10	62	36	2
aged 11–12	69	31	–
aged 13–17	63	36	–
aged 18+	69	31	–

Base: 410 respondents.

Appendix 2: Perceived influences of television

As in previous years, respondents were asked about the influence they thought television might exercise.

Table C

Influence:	Extremely strong %	Strong %	Some %	Much %	None %
Encouraging swearing	17	31	27	17	8
Encouraging aggressive attitudes	12	31	34	15	8
Helping children make sense of social problems	12	30	41	13	4
Encouraging sexual and moral permissiveness	12	24	35	19	9
Making children more inquisitive about their own and other countries	8	27	43	16	6
Brainwashing people	11	19	26	24	20
Lowering children's respect for authority	8	21	34	26	11
Making people accept things they wouldn't normally consider	7	21	45	19	7
Limiting children's imagination	6	19	28	29	18
Helping children to know the difference between right and wrong	4	19	41	25	10
Lowering children's respect for parents	6	15	32	28	19
Encouraging people to think for themselves	4	14	38	29	14

Base: 1137 respondents, all expressing an opinion

In all instances respondents who were over 55 years old were more likely to consider that television had a negative influence on viewers. This was particularly true when they considered television's perceived influence in encouraging swearing (59 per cent of over 55s thought television had an 'extremely strong' or 'strong' influence here in comparison with 48 per cent of the sample as a whole), encouraging aggressive behaviour (61 per cent claimed an influence in comparison with 43 per cent of the total sample) and encouraging sexual and moral permissiveness (57 per cent in comparison with the sample's comment of 36 per cent). In addition this group of respondents were more likely to say that television lowered children's respect for authority and their parents than the sample as a whole.

In contrast, younger respondents were less likely to consider that television's effect was negative and were more likely to say that television had positive benefits. 58 per cent of respondents aged 17 and under were likely to comment on television's importance in making sense of social problems in comparison with 42 per cent of the sample as a whole, and were more likely to consider that television had no influence in encouraging aggression, lowering respect for authority or parents and encouraging sexual and moral permissiveness.

The study did not find that parenthood was a key variable in these results, although a marginally higher proportion of parents said that television played little or no part in encouraging sexual and moral permissiveness. It was also noted that, although the absolute numbers differed between this year and the last, the ranked order of the perceived influence of television remained unchanged.

Appendix 3: The Watershed and warnings

The importance of the Watershed as a guide to the possible nature of programming is well known – 87 per cent of respondents in the quantitative study said that they had heard of it and the majority (two in three) knew that it occurred at 9.00 pm during the week. But there was less certainty about the time of the Watershed at the weekend (which, in fact, is no different from the weekday Watershed). Over one-third of respondents were uncertain whether or not it was different while one quarter of all respondents thought that it was.

Respondents generally thought that different Watershed times should apply for children of different ages and previous research (Millwood Hargrave, 1991) would suggest that parents in particular would agree with this. The 1991 Annual Survey found that parents of children aged 15 and under felt that there should be a distinction made between programming suitable for children who were 9 years old and younger and programming suitable for children older than this. Also, many parents felt that there should be a later Watershed (at 10.00 pm) particularly for children aged between 14 and 15.

Respondents were asked if the Watershed policy would be needed if all programmes had warnings, or information about the material to be included, transmitted before the start of the programme – over three-quarters of the respondents said they thought the policy was still important. Nevertheless, warnings or additional labelling were thought to be useful adjuncts and aids to viewing decisions. Respondents were asked what sort of warnings would be useful to them and the results are set out in Table D.

Table D. Useful symbols for television programming

	%
Spoken warnings before programme begins	73
Written warnings in TV guides or newspapers	65
Cinema and video categories in TV guides or newspapers	60
Cinema and video categories on TV	59
Various symbols in TV guides or newspapers	51
Various symbols on TV	49
None	7

As the Council's research has found in previous years, respondents felt that the most useful guide to a programme's contents was a spoken warning prior to transmission, although a number of respondents suggested that adequate information about the programme within programme guides or listings would also be important.

Appendix 4: Complaints behaviour

Most respondents (96 per cent) said that they had not ever complained about a broadcast on television or radio. Of those who had complained, they had objected to the portrayal of sex (10 per cent), violence (8 per cent), or a particular issue that a programme had raised and with which they disagreed.

If respondents had complained about the sexual content or violence in a programme, they were complaining because they thought there was either too much or they had not had any prior warning.

Thirty-nine per cent of respondents said that they had seen something on the television and had felt like complaining but did not; they had been offended by the sexual content of a programme (28 per cent), the violence (24 per cent), bad language (19 per cent),the overall quality of a programme (15 per cent), or an issue raised (10 per cent).

Four per cent of respondents said that they had felt like complaining about something on the radio but had not done so.

Appendix 5: Methodology

This Review incorporates the results of a qualitative study, conducted by Alison Lyon and Annie Woodhouse of Counterpoint Research, Denis Robb of The Research Practice and David Morrison, Director, Institute of Communication Studies, Leeds University. The results from the qualitative study were used to shape the design of the subsequent quantitative study, conducted by the British Market Research Bureau. An analysis of the content of one week's terrestrial programming was also undertaken. This was carried out by the Communications Research Group at Aston University.

Qualitative study

In structuring the sample there was a desire to encompass a broad cross-section of the population, and to interview this sample within suitable 'peer groups'. There was also a wish to examine the complexities of behaviour and attitudes within family or household units ('family interviews'). In addition, there was a need to talk with those specifically charged with the instruction and care of young people, namely teachers, youth club workers, those involved in social work or employed in residential homes for young people. It was also felt to be important to research the views and opinions of homosexuals on sex and sexuality in broadcasting.

All groups were of 2 hours' duration and were conducted in January and February 1992.

Mainstream 'Peer-group' Sample

Male	16–17 (C1C2)	20–24 (C2D)	25–34 (BC1)	30–45 (C2D)	35–45 (BC1)	55+ (C1C2)
Female	18–19 (C1C2)	20–24 (BC1)	25–35 (C2D)	30–35 (BC1)	35–45 (C2D)	55+ (C1C2)
Criteria	Living with parents	Single, not cohabiting	Married without children	Married, children 5–11 years	Married, children 11–15 years	Empty nesters*

*People with no children living at home

These groups were held in Sheffield, Bristol, Harrow (London), Cambridge/Lincoln-shire borders, Slough and Manchester.

Family interviews

	Children < 7 years	Children 7–11 years	Children 12–15 years	Children 16–19 years
BC1 C2D	Glasgow Thames Valley	London Liverpool	Liverpool London	Thames Valley Nottingham

This technique has been used sucessfully by the Council in previous research. Parents and children are interviewed separately for their opinions and are then brought together for a family interview.

'Carers'

One group discussion was held with residential workers, social workers and community workers with young people, and one group discussion was with teachers, responsible for young people's social, sex and community education. These two groups were held in Glasgow and Nottingham, respectively.

Homosexuals

It was considered important to recruit homosexuals who were not considered 'activists' and who might not normally be asked for their opinions, as homosexuals, about matters. For this reason, a 'snowball' technique was used. Recruiters approached known gays and lesbians and their respective organizations who nominated people not generally canvassed for their views. These homosexuals were then recruited for the research.

Gay group	Gay couple	Lesbian group	Lesbian couple
Nottingham Manchester Middlesex	Nottingham Manchester	Nottingham Manchester Middlesex	Nottingham Manchester

Stimulus material – qualitative study

After respondents' initial attitudes to the transmission of sexual material had been explored, a video tape was shown. This was made up of various excerpts from television programmes and was designed to focus respondents' attention on portrayals of sexual activity. Each clip was put in context by the moderator, who described the nature of the programme, its transmission time, the channel on which it was shown and the scene within which the particular episode was set. Nonetheless, it should be borne in mind that respondents were viewing material out of context, and that the clips were used as aids to discussion only. The order in which the clips were shown reflected the time the programmes would have been broadcast. Each clip was discussed, although some of the material that was broadcast late at night was not shown to younger respondents.

Daytime on Two – Scene: The Two of Us

Two-part drama about teenagers, Phil and Matthew. This first episode deals with Phil, who has a girlfriend, coming to terms with his attraction to Matthew, who is known to be gay. Shown as part of a series of schools programmes to promote discussion on difficult subjects which might affect teenagers.

In this clip Matthew and Phil have been swimming and are in the showers together, with their swimming trunks on. We see them gently touch each other's chest.

Screen One – Ex

Drama in which a television writer is torn between his ex-wife and children and his new actress-girlfriend.

The clip shows him in bed with his girlfriend, under the bed covers. His girlfriend is reluctant to have sex with him because his children are staying and might come in. As they start to kiss the children appear in the doorway, having woken up with nightmares.

Wilt

Adaptation of Tom Sharpe's novel about Henry Wilt. His wife has forced him to go to a party and bored with the company, he starts to wander around the house. He overhears a conversation with his wife and the hostess in the next room and tries to hide, but is found by the hostess who is irritated by him. He gets knocked out by the door frame as he tries to leave the bedroom and the hostess takes her revenge by stripping him naked and tying him to an inflatable 'anatomically correct' doll.

The clip shows Wilt trying to free himself from the inflatable doll.

New Statesman

Situation comedy which centres on the character of Alan B'stard, MP. Shown in an unfavourable light in most episodes, this one shows him at a party in his own house.

The clip shows him in the kitchen having intercourse with his wife over the kitchen table. She uses their intercourse to time the boiling of quails' eggs for the party.

Making Out

Series about factory girls in a Northern city. In this episode Carol is beaten up by her husband and flees to her female boss's house. Although she has known her boss for a long time she knows nothing of her private life.

The clip shows her realizing that her boss's lover is a woman. It later shows the boss and her lover having a conversation while in the bath together.

Smith and Jones

Well-established comedy series. In this sketch Mel Smith is talking about British men's attitudes, and reluctance, to touching each other.

131

The climax of the scene used in the clip shows Mel Smith kissing Griff Rhys Jones fully.

Journey to Knock

A play about a group of people with disabilities who are on a pilgrimage to the holy shrine in Knock in Ireland. The play deals with the attempts of Terry, a young man, to come to terms with a progressive disabling disease.

This clip shows Terry just after he has picked up a girl in a bar and goes home with her. He complains that her flat is on the second floor and that he will not be able to make it up there. The girl attempts to carry him, and having failed, they decide to make love on the stairs. The clip ends with the girl getting cramp in her leg.

Brimstone and Treacle

A play by Dennis Potter in which a young man is taken in as a lodger to a home where the young daughter lies comatose. The clip shows a dream sequence in which the father dreams his daughter is making love to the lodger – in fact, he is muddling it with his own sexual affair with his secretary, which his daughter had happened upon.

Hotel New Hampshire

A film about a family in America who own a hotel. A girl is raped in revenge for humiliating some young men. She is rescued by her brother and friends. Much later the young man who initiated the revenge is humbled.

This clip shows the rape, which takes place in a ditch. Although you cannot see the victim, you can see and hear the mob around her, and the moving body of the rapist.

Sebastiane

A film by Derek Jarman of the story of St Sebastiane. The clip shows a sex scene between two Christian prisoners, being watched over by a Roman guard.

Time to Dance

An adaptation of the novel by Melvyn Bragg describing the obsessive and passionate relationship between a young woman and her older lover. The clip shows the couple making love in an hotel room.

Quantitative study

BMRB was commissioned by the Council to conduct a quantitative survey of attitudes towards the depiction of sex and sexuality among a nationally representative sample. 1038 interviews were carried out throughout England, Scotland, and Wales and a further 99 interviews were carried out in Northern Ireland. 918 of the interviews were with adults aged 18 years or over and 219 with children aged 13 to 17 years. Thus children aged 13-17 were over-sampled as were respondents from Northern Ireland. In both cases, this was to allow sufficient numbers for separate analysis. These boosted samples were down-weighted at the analysis stage to ensure they were in their natural proportions in the total sample.

All interviews were carried out face-to-face and in-home. All interviewers were provided with a comprehensive set of written instructions, detailing who to interview and highlighting any difficult or unusual parts of the questionnaire. Flash cards were used as an integral part of the research.

The main fieldwork was conducted between 6 and 16 April 1992. Average interview length was 50 minutes. The questionnaire was developed during the course of two dynamic piloting stages. The first pilot consisted of 3 days' fieldwork in London and three days in Manchester. The second four-day pilot was conducted in London.

Three versions of the questionnaire were used. Versions 1 and 2, which were asked of adults, were identical except for the rotation of the order of presentation of three written examples of sex scenes and for 3 differing scenarios. Version 3, which was asked of children (aged 13–17), differed from versions 1 and 2 in the three scenarios used and in that it contained no questions about the portrayal of homosexuality on television.

In addition, parental permission was obtained before interviewing any child under the age of 18, due to the sensitivity of the subject.

Sample details

- 69 per cent of the sample had two or more television sets.

- 40 per cent of the sample had children living at home. Of those with children at home, 39 per cent had a television in the child's room.

- VCR penetration was 81 per cent and where children were still living at home, penetration of VCRs was over 90 per cent.

- 2/3 of the sample (67 per cent) timeshifted programmes (recorded off-air) at least once a week.

- 22 per cent of the sample hired or bought pre-recorded video cassettes (PVRCs) at least once a week. This increased to 41 per cent of the under 24 year old sample hiring or buying PVRCs at least once per week.

- 13 per cent of the sample had access to cable or satellite television.

- Of those with cable or satellite film channels (Sky Movies Plus and Sky Movies), 29 per cent claimed to watch them most often. 20 per cent of the male respondents with cable or satellite claimed to watch Sky Sports most often.

- 96 per cent of the sample had a radio and they listened to it, on average, six days per week. The table overleaf shows the profile of radio listeners.

Profile of radio listeners

	Age				Social group			
	13–24	25–34	35–54	55+	AB	C1	C2	DE
R1	44	41	20	3	17	21	32	23
R2	–	2	7	27	9	12	10	10
R3	–	–	2	5	8	2	–	1
R4	2	12	17	21	38	19	4	4
R5	–	3	2	2	2	1	3	2
BBC local	10	11	15	19	9	13	15	18
ILR	31	22	28	17	11	22	29	30
Other	12	9	8	6	5	10	7	12

As the data show, Radio 1 has a significant appeal for the under 35s and Independent Local Radio is even younger in its appeal. The over 55 year old respondent enjoys Radios 2 and 4 and some do listen to BBC local radio. Radio 4 also has an upmarket appeal.

Content analysis

The television output across the four terrestrial channels was recorded from 1800 hours to 2400 hours for seven days from Monday 13 January to Sunday 19 January 1992. The programmes were subjected to a detailed content analysis by trained coders. A schedule of questions had been prepared which asked questions of the programme and its contents. The coding schedules varied in the level of detail captured according to the requirements of each issue (e.g. the depiction of sexual activity, nudity).

Appendix 6: References

Millwood Hargrave, A. (1991): *Taste and Decency in Broadcasting*. John Libbey: London.

Millwood Hargrave, A. (ed.) (1991): *A Matter of Manners? The Limits of Broadcast Language*. John Libbey, London.

Franzblaue, S *et al.* (1977): Sex on TV: A Content Analysis. *Journal of Communication* **27,** (2) pp. 164–170.

Silverman, L. T. *et al.* (1979): Physical Contact and Sexual Behaviour on Prime Time Television. *Journal of Communication* **29,** Winter pp. 33–43.

Greenberg B. *et al.* (1980): Sexual Intimacy on Commercial Television During Prime Time. *Journal Quarterly* 57 (summer) pp. 211–215.

Sprafkin J. N. and Silverman L. T. (1981): Update: Physically Intimate and Sexual Behaviour on Prime Time Television 1978–79. *Journal of Communication* **31,** Winter pp. 34–40.

Greenberg B. *et al.* (1981): Sex on the Soap Operas: Afternoon Delight. *Journal of Communication* **31,** (3) pp. 83–89.

Lowry D. *et al.* (1981): Sex on the Soap Operas: Patterns of Intimacy. *Journal of Communication* **31,** (3) pp. 90–96.

Lowry D. and Towles D. (1989): Soap Opera Portrayals of Sex, Contraception and Sexually Transmitted Diseases. *Journal of Communication* **39,** (2) pp. 76–83.

Greenberg B. *et al.* (1985): Quality and Quantity of Sex in the Soaps. *Journal of Broadcasting and Electronic Media* **23,** No 3, pp. 309–321.

Docherty D., Morrison D., and Tracey M., (1988): *Keeping Faith? Channel 4 and its Audience*. John Libbey: London.

'British Social Attitudes' – The 8th report by Social and Community Planning Research, (1991). Dartmouth Publishing Company Ltd, UK.

Wolf M. A. and Kielwasser A. P. (eds.) (1991): *Gay People, Sex and the Media*. Harrison Park Press, New York.

Appendix 7: Researchers who worked on these projects

Sue Brooker, graduated in History from Exeter University, she has worked at BMRB for 9 years and is Associate Director.

Jonathan Caffrey is a Senior Research Executive at BMRB's Survey Research Division. He has three years' experience in survey research at BMRB.

Dr Guy Cumberbatch is a chartered psychologist who for the last twenty years has specialized in mass communications research. Recent books include *A Measure of Uncertainty*, 1989, Libbey; *Pornography: Impacts and Influences*, 1990, The Home Office; *Television and Disability*, 1991, Routledge. He is Director of the Communications Research Group at Aston University where he teaches Applied Psychology.

Alison Lyon graduated from the University of Strathclyde in 1980, and completed her Doctorate at Leicester University in 1984. From 1983 until 1986 she was Research Officer on a major study of educationally disadvantaged children at Strathclyde University. Since 1986 she has worked as a qualitative researcher, working in media and social research. In March 1991 she set up Counterpoint, a specialist qualitative research consultancy.

Andrea Maguire. Following her first degree in Social Anthropology at Sussex University, Andrea Maguire completed a masters degree at Granada's Centre for Visual Anthropology. Since 1989 she has been research manager of the Communications Research Group where she has been responsible for a wide variety of media studies including content analyses of over 3,000 hours of broadcast television.

Andrea Millwood Hargrave joined the Broadcasting Standards Council as Research Director in February 1991. Previously Director of Planning (Marketing) for British Satellite Broadcasting, she was PREM1ERE's Director of Sales and Marketing and Head of Research for Thorn EMI Cable Programmes and Grampian Television. She graduated from the University of Durham with a Degree in Psychology.

David Morrison is currently Research Director at the Institute of Communication studies at the University of Leeds and special advisor for Media Research at Research International, where he previously worked. He gained his first Degree in Sociology from the University of Hull and his Doctorate in Mass Communication Research from the University of Leicester. He was Research fellow at the University of Leicester and the City University. He is the author of seven books on the media.

Simon Orton, Managing Director of BMRB's Survey Research Division. He has worked at BMRB for almost 20 years, since graduating from Oxford in Politics, Philosophy and Economics.

Helen Pillinger is a Senior Research Executive in BMRB's Survey Research Division, she has 5 years experience in survey research at BMRB.

Denis Robb was born in Ireland and was educated at Queen's University, Belfast, and Cambridge University where he research a PhD on 19th Century political and social attitudes. Denis worked in marketing before becoming an advertising planner in 1978. He set up his own independent qualitative research agency in 1988. In 1990 he became a founding member of The Research Practice, a qualitative research organization.

Jane Wolley is a Research Executive in BMRB's Survey Research Division, she has one years' experience in survey research at BMRB.

Annie Woodhouse was a Senior Lecturer in Sociology at South Bank Polytechnic for 15 years, before switching to market research. During her time at the South Bank, her research centred mainly on sensitive issues, conducting a study of teenage unwanted pregnancy and, more recently a study of transvestism and the effects this has on the wives of transvestites.

Appendix 8: Authors' biographies

Cate Haste is a television director/producer and writer. She has worked as a freelance making documentary films on historical and political subjects for the BBC and ITV companies for over twenty years. These include *The Secret War, The Day Before Yesterday, End of Empire, Just Sex, The Writing on the Wall, Munich – The Peace of Paper*, and recently Channel 4's *Secret History* series. She has published two books *Keep the Home Fires Burning*, on propaganda in the First World War, and, this year, *Rules of Desire*, a social history of the shifts in sexual values and behaviour, private and public, for World War one to the present.

François Hurard, is Head of Programming Services for the Conseil Supérieur de l'Audiovisuel (CSA).

Armando Iannucci read English at University College, Oxford, and stayed on to work on a PhD on Milton and Seventeenth Century Religious Poetry. This led (naturally) to a job as a presenter of a live 'yoof' music and comedy programme on BBC Radio Scotland, while also performing in live comedy. In 1989, he came to London to join the BBC Radio Light Entertainment Department as a Producer taking charge of the likes of *Week Ending, The Mary Whitehouse Experience*, and *The News Quiz*. He originated the Radio One comedy show *Loose Talk* and, for Radio Four, the cult news parody, *On the Hour*. In February 1992 he left the BBC to mix Television and Radio production with writing, broadcasting and live comedy performing.

David Morrison is currently Research Director at the Institute of Communication studies at the University of Leeds and special advisor for Media Research at Research International, where he previously worked. He gained his first Degree in Sociology from the University of Hull and his Doctorate in Mass Communication Research from the University of Leicester. He was Research fellow at the University of Leicester and the City University. He is the author of seven books on the media.

Sally Munt is a Lecturer in Cultural Studies, previously at Brighton Polytechnic, and now at Nottingham Trent University. In 1992 she edited and published *New Lesbian Criticism: Literary and Cultural Readings*, Harvester Wheatsheaf (UK) and Columbia University Press (USA); in 1993 she will be publishing *Murder by the Book: Feminism and the Crime Novel* with Routledge.

Born in Jarrow in 1935, **Alan Plater** was brought up in Hull before training as an architect in Newcastle. He has been a full-time writer since 1961, writing his first plays for radio, a medium which he continues to love. Taking radio, television, theatre and films together, he has over two hundred assorted credits – plus three novels. As a television playwright, he contributed to the pioneering *Z-Cars* and his most recent work includes *Barchester Chronicles*, the *Beiderbecke* trilogy, *Fortunes of War* and *A Very British Coup*. He has won many national and international awards. He has been President of the Writers' Guild of Great Britain since September 1991.

Patrick Stoddart is contributing editor to Broadcast Magazine. He has been television critic of the *Sunday Times*, *Broadcast* and the *London Evening News*, and radio critic of *The Times*. He now works as a freelance journalist and broadcaster.

Sandi Toksvig was born in Copenhagen, Denmark and educated in New York and Girton College, Cambridge. Sandi works both as comic performer and writer. Her television appearances include *Number 73*, *Whose Line is it Anyway?* and *The Big One* (which she co-wrote with Elly Brewer). In 1992 she starred in *The Pocket Dream* (co-written with Elly Brewer and William Shakespeare) in the West End and has just completed a new play for Nottingham Playhouse.

Appendix 9: Publications of the Broadcasting Standards Council

A Code of Practice
November 1989
This publication is available free of charge from the BSC

Broadcasting Standards Council Annual Report 1988–89 and *Code of Practice*
Broadcasting Standards Council Annual Report 1989–90 and *1990–91*
Available from the BSC, £4.00 each

BSC Monograph Series

A Measure of Uncertainty – The Effects of the Mass Media
by Dr Guy Cumberbatch and Dr Dennis Howitt
Co-publishers John Libbey & Co Ltd, 1989, £18.00

Survivors and the Media
by Ann Shearer
Co-publishers John Libbey & Co Ltd, 1991, £10.00

A Matter of Manners? – The Limits of Broadcasting Language
edited by Andrea Millwood Hargrave
Co-publishers John Libbey & Co Ltd, 1991, £12.50

Books

Television and the Public Interest – Vulnerable Values in West European Broadcasting
edited by Professor Jay G Blumler
Published by Sage 1991 £30.00 (Cloth) £11.95 (paper)

Women Viewing Violence: How Women Interpret Violence on Television
Film and Media Research Institute and Institute for the Study of Violence, University of Stirling.
Authors: Professor Philip Schlesinger, Professor Rebecca Dobash, Dr Russell Dobash, Kay Weaver
Published by the BFI 1992 £26.00 (hardback) £10.65 (paperback)

BSC Annual Research Reviews

Public Opinion and Broadcasting Standards – 1
Violence in Television Fiction
by Dr David Docherty
Co-publishers John Libbey & Co Ltd, 1990, £10.00

Public Opinion and Broadcasting Standards – 2
Taste and Decency in Broadcasting
by Andrea Millwood Hargrave
Co-publishers John Libbey & Co Ltd, 1991, £10.00

Public Opinion and Broadcasting Standards – 3
Sex and Sexuality in Broadcasting
by Andrea Millwood Hargrave
Co-publishers John Libbey & Co Ltd, 1992, £12.50

BSC Research Working Papers

I. *Children, Television and Morality, I*
Dr Anne Sheppard, University of Leeds; 1990

II. *Television and Fantasy: An Exploratory study*
The Communications Research Group, Aston University; 1990

III. *Morality, Television and the Pre-adolescent*
Research International, Young Minds; 1990

IV. *Television Advertising and Sex Role Stereotyping*
The Communications Research Group, Aston University; 1990

V. *Children, Television and Morality, II*
Dr Anne Sheppard, University of Leeds; 1992

VI. *Television and Young People*
John Caughie, John Logie Baird Centre, University of Glasgow; 1992

VII. *The Portrayal of Ethnic Minorities on Television*
by Andrea Millwood Hargrave

Working Papers are available from the BSC, £3.00 per copy

Leaflets

Making Complaints
Broadcasting Standards Council and its Activities
Broadcasting and Bad Language

Leaflets available free of charge from the BSC

Future Publications

Understanding Broadcasting – Media Education Across Europe
Editors: David French, Michael Richards. To be published by Routledge.

Children's Television in a Changing Broadcasting System – An Enquiry
by Professor Jay G Blumler

Appendix 10: The Broadcasting Standards Council remit

The Broadcasting Standards Council's remit concerns the portrayal in television and radio programmes and broadcast advertisements of violence, sexual conduct and matters of taste and decency.

The Council was first established on a pre-statutory basis by the Government in May 1988. It became a statutory body under the Broadcasting Act 1990, with effect from 1 January 1991.

The Council has five main tasks:

1. To draw up and from time to time review a Code of Practice in consultation with the broadcasting authorities and others. The Broadcasting Act places a duty on the broadcasters to reflect the BSC's Code in their own codes and programmes guidelines. The BSC's Code was published in November 1989 and circulated widely among broadcasters, interested organizations and members of the public.

2. To monitor programmes and to make reports on the areas within the Council's remit.

3. To commission research into such matters as the nature and effects on attitudes and behaviour of the portrayal of violence and of sex in programmes and advertisements and standards of taste and decency.

4. To consider and make findings on complaints.

5. To represent the UK on international bodies concerned with setting standards for television programmes.

Broadcasting Standards Council
5–8 The Sanctuary
London SW1P 3JS

Tel: 071 233 0544
Fax: 071 233 0397

June 1992

Media titles available from John Libbey

ACAMEDIA RESEARCH MONOGRAPHS

Satellite Television in Western Europe (revised edition 1992)
Richard Collins
Hardback ISBN 0 86196 203 6

Beyond the Berne Convention
Copyright, Broadcasting and the Single European Market
Vincent Porter
Hardback ISBN 0 86196 267 2

The Media Dilemma:
Freedom and Choice or Concentrated Power?
Gareth Locksley
Hardback ISBN 0 86196 230 3

Nuclear Reactions: A Study in Public Issue Television
John Corner, Kay Richardson and Natalie Fenton
Hardback ISBN 0 86196 251 6

Transnationalization of Television in Western Europe
Preben Sepstrup
Hardback ISBN 0 86196 280 X

The People's Voice: Local Radio and Television in Europe
Nick Jankowski, Ole Prehn and James Stappers
Hardback ISBN 0 86196 322 9

Television and the Gulf War
David E. Morrisson
Hardback ISBN 0 86196 341 5

Contra-Flow in Global News
Oliver Boyd Barrett and Daya Kishan Thussu
Hardback ISBN 0 86196 344 X

CNN World Report: Ted Turner's International News Coup
Don M. Flournoy
Hardback ISBN 0 86196 359 8

Small Nations: Big Neighbour
Roger de la Garde, William Gilsdorf and Ilja Wechselmann
Hardback ISBN 0 86196 343 1

BBC ANNUAL REVIEWS

Annual Review of BBC Broadcasting Research: No XV - 1989
Paperback ISBN 0 86196 209 5

Annual Review of BBC Broadcasting Research: No XVI - 1990
Paperback ISBN 0 86196 265 6

Media titles available from John Libbey

Annual Review of BBC Broadcasting Research: No XV - 1991
Paperback ISBN 0 86196 319 9
Peter Menneer (ed)

BROADCASTING STANDARDS COUNCIL PUBLICATIONS

A Measure of Uncertainty: The Effects of the Mass Media
Guy Cumberbatch and Dennis Howitt
Hardback ISBN 0 86196 231 1

Violence in Television Fiction: Public Opinion and Broadcasting Standards
David Docherty
Paperback ISBN 0 86196 284 2

Survivors and the Media
Ann Shearer
Paperback ISBN 0 86196 332 6

Taste and Decency in Broadcasting
Andrea Millwood Hargrave
Paperback ISBN 0 86196 331 8

A Matter of Manners? – The Limits of Broadcast Language
Edited by Andrea Millwood Hargrave
Paperback ISBN 0 86196 337 7

BROADCASTING RESEARCH UNIT MONOGRAPHS

Quality in Television –
Programmes, Programme-makers, Systems
Richard Hoggart (ed)
Paperback ISBN 0 86196 237 0

Keeping Faith? Channel Four and its Audience
David Docherty, David E. Morrison and Michael Tracey
Paperback ISBN 0 86196 158 7

Invisible Citizens:
British Public Opinion and the Future of Broadcasting
David E. Morrison
Paperback ISBN 0 86196 111 0

School Television in Use
Diana Moses and Paul Croll
Paperback ISBN 0 86196 308 3

Media titles available from John Libbey

UNIVERSITY OF MANCHESTER BROADCASTING SYMPOSIUM

And Now for the BBC ...
Proceedings of the 22nd Symposium 1991
Nod Miller and Rod Allen (eds)
Paperback ISBN 0 86196 318 0

Published in association with UNESCO

Video World-Wide: An International Study
Manuel Alvarado (ed)
Paperback ISBN 0 86196 143 9

Published in association with
THE ARTS COUNCIL of GREAT BRITAIN

Picture This: Media Representations of Visual Art and Artists
Philip Hayward (ed)
Paperback ISBN 0 86196 126 9

Culture, Technology and Creativity
Philip Hayward (ed)
Paperback ISBN 0 86196 266 4

ITC TELEVISION RESEARCH MONOGRAPHS

Television in Schools
Robin Moss, Christopher Jones and Barrie Gunter
Hardback ISBN 0 86196 314 8

Television: The Public's View
Barrie Gunter and Carmel McLaughlin
Hardback ISBN 0 86196 348 2

The Reactive Viewer
Barrie Gunter and Mallory Wober
Hardback ISBN 0 86196 358 X

REPORTERS SANS FRONTIÈRES

1992 Report
Freedom of the Press Throughout the World
Paperback ISBN 0 86196 369 5

MEDECINS SANS FRONTIERES

Populations in Danger
François Jean
Paperback ISBN 0 86196 392 X

Media titles available from John Libbey

IBA TELEVISION RESEARCH MONOGRAPHS

Teachers and Television:
A History of the IBA's Educational Fellowship Scheme
Josephine Langham
Hardback ISBN 0 86196 264 8

Godwatching: Viewers, Religion and Television
Michael Svennevig, Ian Haldane, Sharon Spiers and Barrie Gunter
Hardback ISBN 0 86196 198 6
Paperback ISBN 0 86196 199 4

Violence on Television: What the Viewers Think
Barrie Gunter and Mallory Wober
Hardback ISBN 0 86196 171 4
Paperback ISBN 0 86196 172 2

Home Video and the Changing Nature of Television Audience
Mark Levy and Barrie Gunter
Hardback ISBN 0 86196 175 7
Paperback ISBN 0 86196 188 9

Patterns of Teletext Use in the UK
Bradley S. Greenberg and Carolyn A. Lin
Hardback ISBN 0 86196 174 9
Paperback ISBN 0 86196 187 0

Attitudes to Broadcasting Over the Years
Barrie Gunter and Michael Svennevig
Hardback ISBN 0 86196 173 0
Paperback ISBN 0 86196 184 6

Television and Sex Role Stereotyping
Barrie Gunter
Hardback ISBN 0 86196 095 5
Paperback ISBN 0 86196 098 X

Television and the Fear of Crime
Barrie Gunter
Hardback ISBN 0 86196 118 8
Paperback ISBN 0 86196 119 6

Behind and in Front of the Screen - Television's Involvement
with Family Life
Barrie Gunter and Michael Svennevig
Hardback ISBN 0 86196 123 4
Paperback ISBN 0 86196 124 2